Close
Reading
14-16

Comprehension, Interpretation and Language Activities

Mary M Firth
Andrew G Ralston

HODDER
GIBSON
AN HACHETTE UK COMPANY

The Publishers would like to thank the following for permission to reproduce copyright material:

Photo credits Page 11 Andrew Milligan/PA/EMPICS; Page 23 © ACE STOCK LIMITED/Alamy; Page 29 RICK RYCROFT/EMPICS; Page 33 © Artisan/Everett/Rex Features; Page 36 © Topham Picturepoint; Page 41 © Keren Su/China Span/Alamy; Page 45 © 2003 P Kingsford/TopFoto; Page 49 © Medical-on-Line/Alamy; Page 53 KIRKLAND/AP/EMPICS; Page 55 © Tim Graham/Corbis; Page 59 © Tim Graham/Corbis; Page 61 © ROBIN MCKELVIE/Alamy; Page 64 © Steffan Hill/Alamy; Page 67 © DreamWorks Animation/ZUMA/Corbis; Page 70 © Pictorial Press Ltd/Alamy; Page 73 © Content Mine International/Alamy; Page 76 © Roger Williams/ZUMA/ Corbis; Page 79 © Christophe Boisvieux/Corbis; Page 81 Frank Barratt/Keystone/Getty Images; Page 85 © BBC; Page 87 © Harald Woeste/Alamy; Page 91 © David Copeman/Alamy; Page 96 © rollie rodriguez/Alamy; Page 97 UNIVERSAL/THE KOBAL COLLECTION/MC BROOM, BRUCE; Page 100 Rex Features; Page 109 Mirrorpix.

Acknowledgements 'At last! Vindication for working mums' reproduced with the permission of NI Syndication; 'There's s-no Xscape' reproduced with the permission of The Sunday Herald © Newsquest (Herald & Times) Ltd; 'Solved: Why women obsess about their food more than men' reproduced with the permission of Express Syndication; 'In our own words: What it's like to be a teenager' reproduced with the permission of NI Syndication; 'Right out the blue' reproduced with the permission of The Sunday Herald © Newsquest (Herald & Times) Ltd; 'Horror movies are nothing on my dark mind' reproduced by permission of The Telegraph; 'Taking the Train to Windsor' © Bill Bryson. Extracted from NOTES FROM A SMALL ISLAND by Bill Bryson, published by Black Swan, a division of Transworld Publishers. All rights reserved; 'There are 14 doctor dramas on TV right now...' reproduced with the permission of NI Syndication; 'Dare, kiss or promise? How Elizabeth II chose the last' reproduced by permission of The Telegraph; 'Bargain on the Orient Express' reproduced with the permission of The Daily Mail; 'Gromit has a grand day out' reproduced by permission of The Telegraph; 'The young hero of Macauley Culkin's novel...' Excerpt from "Young Adult Fiction" by David Amsden. New York Magazine, 3/13/06; 'A life lived on the edge' reproduced with the permission of The Daily Mail; 'Germany's grown up, now it's your turn' reproduced by permission of The Telegraph; 'Living History: A timeless city' by Catherine Nixey. Published in 'UK Life', Issue 2, Winter 2003. Copyright Independent News and Media Limited; 'Eat Up and Pay Up' reproduced with the permission of The Daily Mail; 'Chav-Air cheapens the thrill of travel' reproduced by permission of The Telegraph; 'Nothing, and I mean nothing, is better value than this' reproduced with the permission of NI Syndication.

Every effort has been made to trace all copyright holders, but if any have been inadvertently overlooked the Publishers will be pleased to make the necessary arrangements at the first opportunity.

Although every effort has been made to ensure that website addresses are correct at time of going to press, Hodder Gibson cannot be held responsible for the content of any website mentioned in this book. It is sometimes possible to find a relocated web page by typing in the address of the home page for a website in the URL window of your browser.

Hachette's policy is to use papers that are natural, renewable and recyclable products and made from wood grown in sustainable forests. The logging and manufacturing processes are expected to conform to the environmental regulations of the country of origin.

Orders: please contact Bookpoint Ltd, 130 Milton Park, Abingdon, Oxon OX14 4SB. Telephone: (44) 01235 827720. Fax: (44) 01235 400454. Lines are open 9.00–5.00, Monday to Saturday, with a 24-hour message answering service. Visit our website at www.hoddereducation.co.uk. Hodder Gibson can be contacted direct on: Tel: 0141 848 1609; Fax: 0141 889 6315; email: hoddergibson@hodder.co.uk

© Mary M Firth and Andrew G Ralston 2007
First published in 2007 by
Hodder Gibson, an imprint of Hodder Education,
an Hachette UK company
2a Christie Street
Paisley PA1 1NB

ISBN-13: 978-0-340-94014-3
Impression number   6
Year 2012

ISBN-13: 978-0340-94015-0 (With Answers)
Impression number   5
Year 2011

Cover photo Clockwise from top right: © Design Pics Inc. / Alamy; © istockphoto/Adrian Hughes; © istockphoto.com/Tadija Savic; © istockphoto.com/Carmen Martínez
Illustrations by Richard Duszczak, Cartoon Studio Limited
Typeset in 10 on 13.5pt Stone Serif by Phoenix Photosetting, Chatham, Kent
Printed in India

A catalogue record for this title is available from the British Library

Contents

Getting Started

What on earth can I do to prepare for the Close Reading paper ...?

Well, let's deal with Close Reading papers first, which you get in Intermediate 2 and Higher exams. For the Reading Exams you get at Standard Grade, look at Page 6!

Everyone says the Close Reading paper is the worst part of the exam. Is it more difficult than the Critical Essay paper?

Students are often nervous because they know they will have to answer questions on a piece of writing they have not seen before. However, there are ways to prepare that will make this part of the exam less daunting. For example, you can work through the questions in past papers.

What is the point of doing past papers since we will get different passages and different questions?

Practising past papers is useful in many ways; for example, in learning how to manage your time. It will also help you recognise certain types of questions that are often asked. You can learn how to approach the different types, and the most likely ways of gaining marks. And you will see that the passages do have a lot in common, too.

What kind of passage are we likely to get?

Firstly, it will be *non-fiction*. Unlike the prose passages in Textual Analysis, the Close Reading passage will be factual. It may present ideas and arguments on a current topic of interest. A recent paper looked at how to make science more popular. Alternatively, it may be an account of a writer's personal experience. For example, in another paper the writer was describing a boat journey he had taken down the Mississippi.

Secondly, the passage will have been chosen to be *entertaining*. Many of the passages are taken from popular newspapers. Journalists must attract and capture the interest of their readers. Most often they do so by being funny, or by using an informal, witty, chatty style. However, they may aim to captivate the audience in more serious ways, for example by being dramatic or emotional. As well as grasping the meaning, you must aim to pick up on the writer's tone.

What kinds of questions will we be asked?

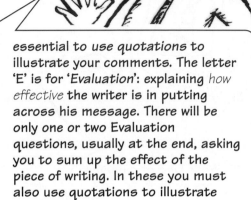

Most importantly, you should look at the code letter after each question. 'U' stands for 'Understanding'. These questions test if you know *what* the writer is saying. The important thing in these questions is to use your own words. The key 'A' stands for 'Analysis'. You will be asked to comment on *how* the writer has expressed the ideas. As you will have to explain how the writer has used language, it will be essential to use quotations to illustrate your comments. The letter 'E' is for '*Evaluation*': explaining *how effective* the writer is in putting across his message. There will be only one or two Evaluation questions, usually at the end, asking you to sum up the effect of the piece of writing. In these you must also use quotations to illustrate your comments.

So how do you make sure you get good marks?

To begin with, here are some things that don't affect the marks! Firstly, there is no need to repeat the words of the questions in your answers. It just wastes time. Secondly, don't repeat yourself or write too much in questions worth only 1 or 2 marks. Thirdly, don't spend time worrying over your *own* spelling and expression.

As long as your answers can be understood, you won't lose marks for language errors. In many questions you don't even need to write in sentences — note form or bullet points will do. Of course, if you are explaining something, which is the case in Analysis and Evaluation questions, you will make yourself clearer if you write in sentences.

Are there any other tips for getting marks?

Yes. There are recommended methods – almost like formulae – for answering certain types of question. These include the so-called 'context' questions, where you must explain what a word means from its placing in the passage, or questions on linkage. Questions on imagery, word choice and sentence structure should also be approached in a particular way. Each of the practice papers in this book will be followed by advice on how to answer a particular type of question.

So, if we learn the formulae, will we pass?

It should certainly help! However, English is not like a science, and you must think about each question individually. There are also two more tips which you should always keep in mind.

Always provide some sort of answer – guess if necessary. A blank space will never gain any marks.

Watch your time! It's important to get down an answer to every question, even if it means writing in note form. Any question left unanswered will always score zero!

A lot of the advice that's just been given applies to Standard Grade Reading Exams as well, but please remember that in Standard Grade the passages can be from fiction (or any genre) as well as non-fiction. Also, in Standard Grade the questions do not have code letters 'U', 'A' and 'E' after them. The rest of this book uses these terms and continues to provide non-fiction passages for practice so that you will be better prepared for the future at either Intermediate 2 or Higher – but you should also be extremely well-prepared for Standard Grade as well!

Writing in Focus 1

Sitting reading a newspaper might not seem like working!

In fact, it is one of the best ways to improve your understanding of written English.

Remember that most Close Reading passages in Intermediate and Higher English exams are written by journalists.

You should train yourself to be able to identify these language features:

- Different registers (i.e. formal and informal language; dialect; jargon)
- Different kinds of sentence structures (lists; build-up to climax; use of colons, semi-colons and dashes)
- Paragraph construction (e.g. the use of topic sentences and linking methods)
- Imagery (particularly similes and metaphors)
- Other special effects (alliteration, onomatopoeia, etc.)
- Rhetorical questions
- Tone (humorous, serious, ironic, etc.)
- Exaggeration (hyperbole)
- Effective word choice.

For practice

Working in pairs or groups, discuss how effectively these techniques are used in the newspaper article that follows.

To help you, some examples of language techniques have been underlined and explanations of some of the words are given in the footnotes.

- First of all, identify which technique is being used in each of the underlined examples.

- Then discuss what you think the writer achieves by using these methods. For example, a writer may use a particular technique for one or more of these reasons:
  - to involve the reader
  - to create humour
  - to convey information
  - to create a descriptive effect
  - to make a link from one point to another
  - to stress the importance of something.

In the following article, journalist Carol Midgley comments on a report which claims that women who combine a full-time job with bringing up children may actually be improving their chances of a healthy life.

Extract

At Last! Vindication[1] for Working Mums

1　Well knock me down with an anti-static feather duster. Working mothers, also known as multi-tasking whirling dervishes[2] who daily burn off more (nervous) energy than a NASA rocket launcher, tend to become less fat and less ill than those who stay at home.

5　　Could anything be more obvious? When does someone who leaves the house at a run every day while scratching chocolate spread from her skirt, who spends her lunch breaks speed-shopping at Tesco and doing furtive[3] internet research for her children's homework projects, all the while trying to earn a living, ever get the chance to pile on pounds?

10　As for getting ill, well it's not really an option. It's tempting to cite research here showing that being at home all day can make women feel lonely and depressed while paid employment boosts self-esteem and thus the immune system. But the truth is probably that working mothers are too turbo-charged with adrenalin to notice the symptoms of even the Ebola virus.

15　　I'm not suggesting that stay-at-home mothers (SAHMs) sit watching TV all day with a pack of Chocolate Hobnobs (though that would be my goal). Holding down a job is undoubtedly less knackering than chasing children around for 14 hours a day. But SAHMs do have permanent access to a fridge, something that I found challenging during my maternity leave as it drew me

20　towards it like a wasp to a dollop of jam.

Extract continued

If SAHMs are feeling poorly they visit the doctor. Working mothers exist in a state of denial, believing that anything can be <u>nuked</u> by industrial amounts of Nurofen Plus. Secretly, they think that unless they are <u>firing on all cylinders</u> civilisation will fall apart.

25   If this sounds faintly smug that's probably because it is. Not only because it confounds all those <u>deeply irritating</u> surveys that claim that 'housework burns off more calories than a workout at the gym!', usually accompanied by a picture of an 18-inch waisted 1950s housewife, but also because working mothers are more <u>pilloried</u>[4] than at any time in history. Piling on our guilt has become a

30   national sport.

    You can't blame us for gloating on the rare occasions that we <u>score a goal.</u>

[1] Vindication: justification; proving someone was right
[2] Whirling dervish: a Muslim holy man who performs a whirling dance to reach a state of religious ecstasy
[3] Furtive: sly, guilty, secretive
[4] Pillory: wooden frame with holes for the head and hands of a guilty person who is then exposed to public ridicule

Chapter 1

There's S-no Xscape

In this article, Edd McCracken describes how Glasgow's Sno Zone offers young people the chance to improve their snowboarding skills all year round.

Extract

1   It's the hottest day of the year. Like over-excited footballers, the good people of Glasgow are celebrating by shedding their clothes. Builders work on their lobster-red tans, while young men walk down Buchanan Street dazzling passers-by with their porcelain torsos. The Clyde looks almost swimmable – it's
5   that hot.

   Considering these extraordinary circumstances, spending today inside a giant fridge where the temperature never creeps above −5° is rather perverse. But that's where I find myself, snowboarding inside Xscape's Sno Zone in Braehead. On real snow.
10   My guide through this faux-winter wonderland is ten-year-old championship skier and snowboarder Nicole Ritchie. Nicole is already a regular at Sno Zone. Within five minutes of meeting, she's throwing snowballs at me while we are on the lift.

Extract continued

'The snow is really good here – it tastes exactly the same as real snow too,
15 very nice,' she says, this time sucking on a snowball, as opposed to throwing it.
Nicole should know: she's trained at the British Ski Team camp in the Alps and
has a room full of trophies and awards. In some ways, the Sno Zone is better
than the mountains, she says.

'The snow here is like real snow, but if the snow wears away, there's
20 artificial surface underneath, so you can still keep going whereas, on the
mountain, if the snow wears away, you can't keep going. It's just rocks. The
Austrians can't train at the moment because there's no snow there, but we've
got an indoor place.'

It snows every night at Braehead. A total of sixteen snow guns fire cooled
25 water into air chilled to –2° making 1700 tonnes of real snow to cover the 200m
slope and the 50m nursery slope, the biggest in the UK.

Sadly, you can't just launch yourself onto the piste. For safety reasons you
need to be able to control your speed, link a turn and use the Poma lift before
the staff will let you run riot. But fret not, lessons are available on the smaller
30 50m slope to bring you up to scratch.

Nicole doesn't need any lessons. She whizzes up and down the slope, over
the rails and table tops, doing jumps and putting people three times her age to
shame.

Pete Kelly has nothing to fear from Nicole yet. He grinds down one of the
35 rails, creating enough heat in this ice box to send sparks flying, before doing a
360 over a jump. He is in awe of the younger kids whizzing about the slope.

'It's the same with any sport – start young, grow up to be a genius,' he says.
'Some of the kids can bounce and flex, unlike older people. Young people
bounce, old people break.'

40 As ever, the continuous sound track to the frosty festivities is rib-shuddering
hip-hop, its relaxed bass thud the perfect accompaniment to a sport that is
devilishly hard to make look laid-back and easy. There's a healthy mix of dare-
devils busting extreme moves, with plenty of people taking baby steps (more
like stumbles) off the table tops.

45 Families look in from behind the glass, their faces a mixture of wonder and
bemusement as they gaze at a mini-Narnia scene, hidden in the corner of a retail
park just outside Glasgow. From the slopes, it's like being a performing dolphin
on the inside of an aquarium.

The session draws to a close. The boarders make their way outside into the
50 balmy air. Snowboard boots are swapped for sandals and baggy trousers for
baggy shorts. Amongst them all the excited chatter is the same – it's going to
be a long, cold summer.

Questions

1   The writer creates various contrasts between paragraphs one and two. In your own words, explain **one** example of these contrasts.   **2 A**

2   In paragraph one (lines 1–5) the author uses imagery (similes and metaphors) to suggest that Glasgow people are not used to hot weather. Choose any **two** of these images and explain how effective you find them.   **4 A/E**

3   'On real snow' (line 9). How appropriate do you find this sentence as a conclusion to paragraph two?   **2 A**

4   Quote the word from paragraph two (lines 6–9) which describes the writer's feelings about the idea of snowboarding on a hot day.   **1 U**

5   In your own words, explain **two** pieces of evidence from paragraph 4 (lines 14–18) which show that ten-year-old Nicole Ritchie is an expert skier and snowboarder.   **2 U**

6   In your own words, explain why Nicole Ritchie believes that 'In some ways, the Sno Zone is better than the mountains' (lines 17–18).   **2 U**

7   'It snows every night at Braehead' (line 24). Show how the sentence that follows (lines 24–26) expands on this statement.   **2 A**

8   'Nicole doesn't need any lessons' (line 31). Show how this sentence forms a link between the previous paragraph and the one that follows.   **2 A**

9   In your own words, explain one way in which Pete Kelly considers young people to have an advantage when it comes to ski-ing and snowboarding.   **2 U**

10 a)   In paragraph 11 (lines 40–44) the writer describes the different types of people who take part in snowboarding at the Sno Zone. Show how his word choice is effective in conveying
    (i)   the risks taken by the more experienced
    (ii) the beginners' lack of skill.   **4 A**

    b)   Quote the expression that conveys the writer's attitude to the fact that both skilled and unskilled snowboarders are taking part.   **1 U**

11 Read paragraph 12 (lines 45–48). Comment on any aspects of the word choice and imagery that you find helpful in conveying to the reader (a) what the scene looks like to the spectators behind the glass and (b) how those on the slopes feel about the spectators.   **4 A**

12 In what ways might the last sentence be considered an appropriate conclusion to this article?   **2 E**

TOTAL MARKS: 30

Taking a closer look ...

Showing 'Understanding'

Questions marked 'U' for Understanding are simply testing whether you know
what a writer means. Sometimes these questions will test your knowledge of
single words or expressions, as in the case of question 10b, where the answer
was 'a healthy mix'.

For practice (1)

Quote a word or expression from the passage which corresponds to each of the
following definitions. The lines where the answer is to be found are given in
brackets.

1 pale, like fine china (lines 1–5)
2 contrary (lines 6–9)
3 fake (lines 10–13)
4 specially prepared slope (lines 27–30)
5 worry (lines 27–30)
6 respect (lines 34–36)
7 bend (lines 37–39)
8 puzzlement (lines 45–48)
9 shopping centre (lines 45–48)
10 warm and still (lines 49–52)

Finding evidence

Other questions test your understanding by asking for 'evidence'. You will
almost always be told which lines of the passage contain the 'evidence'. What
you must do is find the information in these lines which shows that you
understand what the writer means. You should then express this, using your
own words as far as possible.

Remember to look carefully at the number of marks in the question. Sometimes
the questions will tell you how many pieces of 'evidence' you must give. If not,
try to write down **one** piece of evidence for each available mark.

Question 5 above was an example of this type of question. You were asked to
explain **two** pieces of evidence from lines 14–18 which showed that Nicole
Ritchie was an expert skier and snowboarder. The words that contained this
evidence were 'championship'; 'trained at the British Ski Team camp' and 'room
full of trophies and awards'.

> **Tip:** Use your own words! If you were to copy these words straight from the passage
> without further explanation you would be unlikely to get any marks.

A good answer might have read like this:

> One piece of evidence that she is an expert is that she is a 'championship' skier, which means she competes at the top level. This is confirmed by the information that she trains with the British Ski Team, who are the best in the country. A second piece of evidence is the large number of prizes in her room showing she has won many competitions.

For practice (2)

Answer the following additional 'Understanding' questions, making sure that you present the 'evidence' in your own words.

1 Explain **two** pieces of evidence from lines 10–23 which show that Nicole Ritchie was confident and relaxed with the writer.
2 Explain **two** pieces of evidence from the first half of the passage (lines 1–26) that tell the reader Sno Zone is extremely large.
3 Explain **two** pieces of evidence from lines 27–30 that tell the reader the staff at Sno Zone are very safety-conscious.
4 Explain **two** pieces of evidence from lines 34–36 that tell the reader Pete Kelly is a top-class snowboarder.
5 Explain **two** pieces of evidence from lines 40–44 that tell the reader the background music at Sno Zone is very loud.

Chapter 2

Solved: Why Women Obsess about their Food more than Men

Jo Macfarlane describes new research which sheds some light on why men and women react to food in different ways.

Extract

1　If a woman is tempted into having an extra slice of cake, don't blame it on greed, blame it on her brain.

　　Scientists have found that women's brains react to food very differently – and much more strongly – than men's. Academics found that decades of dieting
5　pressure on women and advertising have programmed certain parts of the female brain to go into stimulation when faced with any kind of food. Chocolate is a guilty pleasure and counting calories a feature of daily life for many women.

　　Men, on the other hand, are not usually as obsessive about what they eat.
10　Women may even be biologically conditioned to react differently to food. The research also explains why they are more likely to diet – because they are constantly trying to justify whatever they eat.

　　Dr Rudolf Uher and his colleagues at King's College London Institute of Psychiatry used brain scanning technology, known as functional magnetic
15　resonance imaging (fMRI), to look at the brains of eighteen men and women.

➤

Some of the people in the sample had eaten normally and others had been asked to fast for the previous twenty-four hours. The volunteers were given images of food to look at, as well as food to taste. Their brain reactions were monitored by the scientists.

20 They found that the occipitotemporal cortex – the area of the brain that monitors and reflects how other parts of the brain react to the food – registered the strongest activity. And the female brains reacted much more strongly than their male counterparts.

The same reaction did not happen when they were shown non-food images. 25 The team believe this means women think more about food than men tend to do. They also make more decisions about whether they should eat it.

Dr Uher told *New Scientist* magazine: 'This could be related to biological differences between men and women. But the more likely explanation is that women have a more complicated reaction to food because of social pressure.'

30 Dr Uher's research group is now extending its study to look at patients with eating disorders and obesity. Professor Carey Cooper, psychology and health professor at Lancaster University, said: 'I think they're really on to something with this. For centuries women have had a providing role – preparing and cooking food for their families. And it's part of that role to make sure the food 35 is safe. They will therefore be much more sensitive to food than men are, and I would not be surprised if that was now built into their DNA. If the female brain reacts to food because it historically has developed neural pathways to do this, then food will be the way they express their stress. Food is a neurological stimulant for women, and a comfort.'

40 But other experts have warned that more research must be done before the results can be confirmed. American scientist Angelo del Parigi of the John B. Pierce Laboratory in New Haven, Connecticut, said: 'Looking at an fMRI alone cannot confirm whether the stronger reaction in women is due to innate differences or a learned process.'

Questions

1 Explain clearly **one** way in which the title of the article is appropriate.   2 A

2 Quote the words from paragraph one which best sum up the main point the writer is making in this article.   1 U

3 Comment on the effectiveness of the expression 'decades of dieting pressure' (lines 4–5).   2 A

4   Look again at lines 6–9.
    In your own words, explain the main difference between men's and
    women's attitudes to food.   **2 U**

5   Explain the function of the dash in line 11.   **2 A**

6   In your own words, state the main findings of the experiments carried
    out by Dr Rudolf Uher using brain scanning technology.   **2 U**

7   a)   The writer employs technical **jargon** at some points in the passage.
         Quote **two** examples of this kind of language.   **1 A**

    b)   Comment on the effectiveness of the author's use of such
         expressions.   **2 A**

8   Look again at lines 27–29.

    a)   In your own words, state the two alternative explanations of why
         men and women react to food differently.   **2 U**

    b)   Which of these explanations does Dr Uher find more convincing?   **1 U**

    c)   Quote an expression that tells you this.   **1 A**

9   a)   Quote an expression from lines 30–39 that shows Professor Carey
         Cooper's view of the research findings.   **1 U**

    b)   Explain how the author establishes a conversational tone here.   **1 A**

10 Show how the sentence 'But other experts . . . can be confirmed'
    (lines 40–41) provides a link between the previous paragraph and the
    one that follows.   **2 A**

11 To what extent does American scientist Angelo del Parigi support the
    research findings of Dr Uher?   **2 U**

12 Give the meaning of the word 'innate' (line 43) and explain how the
    rest of the sentence helps you to work this out.   **2 A**

13 By referring to any **two** techniques used in the passage, comment on
    how convincing you find the author's argument.   **4 E**

TOTAL MARKS: **30**

Taking a closer look . . .

Punctuation: colons, semi-colons and dashes

Students often confuse the colon and semi-colon. A colon is made up of two
dots (:) and a semi-colon combines a dot and a comma (;).

They each have different functions.

- **A colon** introduces a quotation. For example, line 27 of the passage says:
  Dr Uher told New Scientist *magazine: 'This could be related to biological differences between men and women.'*

  A colon can also be used to introduce a list or an explanation:
  There can only be one explanation of his behaviour: he is completely mad.

- **A semi-colon** marks the end of a sentence, but less firmly than a full stop does. It is most often used where a sentence is closely related to the one that follows it. For example, the second one might provide a contrast or balance to the previous one.
  My parents like to get up early at the weekend; I would rather have a long lie.

  Remember: when a semi-colon is used it would often be quite acceptable to put a full stop instead, but it would be wrong to put a comma.

A **dash** can be used in a similar way to a colon – to introduce an explanation. The writer does this in lines 33–34:
For centuries women have had a providing role – preparing and cooking food for their families.

Two dashes can be used to mark off an extra piece of information in the middle of a sentence, a technique known as **parenthesis.** The writer uses this technique in lines 20–22.
They found that the occipitotemporal cortex – the area of the brain that monitors and reflects how other parts of the brain react to food – registered the strongest activity.

A definition of the technical medical term is given between the dashes.

For practice

Read the following extracts.

Identify examples of dashes, colons and semi-colons and discuss the purposes for which these are used.

a)

1   Every computer games player has dreamt of working in the electronic games industry. If you are one of those, now might be your chance to shine: the market is booming and companies need all the gifted people they can get.
    But creating fantastic games takes more than just programming; platforms
5   are becoming more powerful by the day and consumers' expectations have grown – increasing the demand for cutting-edge artwork, graphics and sound.
    If you are passionate about games and would rather be saving – or destroying! – the world on your computer than anything else, that's a good start to your career. Ken Levine, CEO and creative director of US developer
10 Irrational Games, says: 'If you are going to come home from your job or school at night and spend your spare time preparing game mods – customised modifications – it's because you are passionate about games.'

b)

1   Futuroscope is France's second largest attraction after – you guessed it – Disneyland. There's plenty to see and do but it's most famous for its five vast cinemas and gut-churning simulator rides that use Imax technology. The 450-seater Kinema cinema has a shimmering, spiky outside; inside, it houses one of
5   the world's largest flat movie screens – 30 metres high!
    The Magic Carpet Cinema was designed to look like a bunch of optical fibres – but it looks more like a huge church organ. Inside, things get even more weird: sitting in one of the 250 luxurious armchair seats I found myself staring at a giant 672 m^2 screen. As the film started rolling, I was glad of one thing: that
10 I hadn't stuffed myself at lunchtime. The IMAX Magic Carpet system uses Double IMAX technology: two films are projected simultaneously from two separate projection rooms, one above and one below – a very clever way of totally immersing you in a 2D film.

Chapter 3

Teenagers

What is it like to be a teenager? Journalist Penny Wark contacted 500 young people to find out. The results of her experiment surprised her . . .

Extract

1   It occurred to us one day that we didn't know what teenagers are like. We know what we think they are like, we know all the clichés, and we know what we were like at that age. But however amusing it is to propagate the notion that teenagers grunt and slouch and get cross and go red and qualify as little more than a sub-
5   species that might one day grow into humans, we suspected that there was more to them than that, and that we ought to try to understand them better.

So we invited teenagers to write to us, explaining what it feels like to be them. We received more than 500 responses, some angry, some sad, many raw and all fiercely articulate about the complex condition of being stuck in the
10   hinterland between childhood and fully fledged adulthood.

At the same time I travelled around Britain, talking to dozens of teenagers I had never met before. Not one was remotely like Harry Enfield's Kevin the teenager and – shock, horror – many were pleasant, well-adjusted young people feeling their way sensibly, and sometimes a little stupidly, through adolescence.
15   As one should.

Extract continued

But there were others who were clearly troubled. Some I found myself mentoring, telling them that things would get better. Some moved me profoundly, making me want to protect them even though I knew that I couldn't, and that it would be dishonest to pretend that I could. It struck me that
20 their most immediate need was a good hug, and that was the problem: there was no one in their family who cared for them enough to notice.

What did I discover? That a teenager who has loving, caring, supportive and unselfish parents will, eventually in some cases, cope. That a teenager who has one loving, caring, supportive and unselfish parent will also cope. And that
25 there are a significant number of teenagers whose parents are either physically or emotionally absent from their children, or both, and these teenagers will struggle and may fail.

So while it is obvious that parenting matters, it's clear that just as there are some disadvantaged mothers who have children with little thought for their
30 welfare, and who neglect their children from the day they are born, there are also plenty of middle-class parents who are too self-absorbed to put in place the barriers that make children feel safe. Asian families tend not to be among them: six of the 36 teenagers I interviewed are Asian and each was remarkably calm – sorted, they would say. Their families are strong and structured, they live in a
35 defined community and their religious faith means that many of the complications teenagers feel they need to address – sex, drinking, drug taking – are not options, so they don't have to worry about them. And they don't.

Looking at the written and verbal accounts of teenagerdom together, one more thing emerged. Teenagers hate being stereotyped. They hate adults who
40 tell them what they are like and how they feel: they want to have their say without adult filtering or analysis.

Questions

1 In paragraph one the author describes what many people think of teenagers.

   a)   In your own words, state what this opinion is.   **1 U**

   b)   Justify your answer by giving **two** close references to the passage.   **2 A**

2 Quote an expression that shows the writer does not share this view.   **1 A**

3 Look at lines 7–10.
The writer talks of teenagers as 'being stuck in the hinterland between childhood and fully fledged adulthood.'

a) Explain what she means by this.   **1 U**

b) Choose one example of the author's word choice in this sentence and explain how it helps you to understand the point she is making.   **2 A**

4 Find a word from paragraph two (lines 7–10) that means 'able to express your opinion in a fluent way.'   **1 U**

5 a) What conclusion did the author come to after travelling round Britain talking to teenagers? (lines 11–15).   **2 U**

b) How does her use of punctuation show that she was surprised by what she found?   **2 A**

6 Read lines 16–21.

a) What does the writer identify as the main thing lacking in many teenagers' lives?   **1 U**

b) Explain the function of the colon in line 20.   **2 A**

7 'What did I discover?' (Line 22).
Comment on the importance of this sentence in the development of the argument of the whole passage.   **2 A**

8 The phrase 'physically or emotionally absent' (lines 25–26) means:

a) the parents are never at home

b) the parents are at home but do not show much affection to their son or daughter

c) both of the above.   **1 U**

9 Read lines 28–37.

In your own words, explain the ways in which the author considers (a) 'some disadvantaged mothers' and (b) 'plenty of middle-class parents' contribute to the problems experienced by their children.   **4 U**

10 In your own words, explain **two** reasons why the author thinks that teenagers from Asian families feel more secure.   **2 U**

11 How effective is the author's use of the word 'sorted' (line 34)?   **2 A**

12 'Teenagers hate being stereotyped' (line 39).
Give the meaning of 'stereotyped' and explain how the rest of the sentence helps you to work it out.   **2 A**

13 The author states that her aim in this passage was 'to try to understand [teenagers] better'. Comment on how successful you feel she has been in achieving this purpose.   **2 E**

TOTAL MARKS: 30

Taking a closer look . . .

Formal and informal language

The spoken English used in everyday conversation can be described as **informal** language. We use

- Shortened forms of words (abbreviations) like *don't, can't, isn't, etc.*
- Slang expressions
- Personal pronouns like *I* and *you.*

I think he's really cool, don't you?

Written language tends to be more **formal**.

- Shortened forms are written in full *(do not, cannot, is not).*
- The word choice will be more precise, correct and perhaps more complicated.
- The tone will not be chatty or personal.
- There will be more emphasis on information and ideas rather than on feelings.

For practice (1)

The passage on Teenagers makes use of both formal and informal language (sometimes referred to as **register**).

- Draw up two columns.
- Head one 'formal' and the other 'informal'.
- Then write out the following phrases under the heading you think describes each one best.

Even though I knew that I couldn't

What did I discover?

Propagate the notion

Physically or emotionally absent

They don't have to worry about them

They live in a defined community

Sorted

Adult filtering or analysis

Their families are strong and structured

Shock, horror

And they don't

For practice (2)

In pairs or groups, discuss the style of the following extracts. Decide which ones are formal and which ones are informal, and identify the language features that help you to decide. (Note that an extract is not necessarily completely formal or completely informal. Writers often use a combination of registers.)

a) Picture this: you're aboard a luxurious cruise ship somewhere in the north Atlantic, it's New Year's Eve, you're happy and the vibe is good. Then a huge wave crashes into the ship. It jolts, turns upside down and you're thrown from the floor to the ceiling! That's what happens to the tonnes of rich folk and crew aboard the *Poseidon*. We're talking total disaster as bodies are flung out to sea, crushed and burned. The captain wants the survivors to stay put and wait to be rescued but a small group think that's nuts and the only way to survive is to find a way off the ship before it sinks.

b) Tetrodotoxin is one of the strongest poisons on the planet – 10,000 times more deadly than cyanide. It's found in poison arrow frogs, puffer fish, and the beautiful but deadly blue ringed octopus. It kills by stopping the lungs working. Consequently, victims suffocate and their lips and tongue turn blue. Weight for weight it is 100 times more lethal than black widow spider venom. The amount of poison in one puffer fish alone could kill thirty people and there is no antidote.

c) So, just how personal is your personal computer? Does the background pic show your fave celeb, or just the big green field that Microsoft put there?

Personalising your PC is easy. You can ditch the bland background and get a proper pic in place.

In fact, it's so easy on Windows XP, you'll wonder why you didn't do it before. The hard part is actually choosing a pic in the first place. Some sites have tons of pics you can use. There are plenty of fan sites for celebs and bands where you can download screen-sized pics. And for all-round personalisation, why not download a wallpaper to your phone while you're at it?

d)   People only bother to learn to calculate stuff like forces, impact speeds and momentum to pass their science exams at school, right? Wrong. If you're strapped into a Formula One car hurtling round a circuit at over 200 mph, you'll want to know the engineers and designers have worked out exactly how it will respond if it suddenly comes off the track or smashes into one of its competitors.

However, motor racing isn't the only sport in which collisions of one sort or another are likely. Some of these impacts are accidental, while others are essential to the sport. After all, it would be a boring game of football if there was no tackling.

For practice (3)

Cut out an article from a newspaper or magazine that you read. Decide whether it is written in a formal or informal style, or a mixture of both. Underline some examples of these different styles.

Chapter 4

Right out of the Blue

Awash with talent, young Scots swimmers are lengths ahead of the rest of the UK.

Extract

1   Think of Scottish sporting success and you'll be thinking for a long time. There's been the occasional, glorious spark in football, such as Celtic winning the European Cup in 1967, Archie Gemmill's goal in 1978, or Aberdeen winning the Cup Winner's Cup in 1983, but this is ancient history. Likewise,
5   Alan Wells, our Olympic champion in the ultimate athletic discipline, the 100m, won that title over a quarter of a century ago. Rugby grand slams have been absent from these parts since 1990.

   All of which makes what happened in Melbourne in March 2006 even more startling. Put simply, Scotland ruled the pool at the Commonwealth Games.
10   Australia may have won the most medals as expected, but the big story was Scotland walking away with twelve medals, six of which were gold.

   'The Australians' reaction was of immediate shock, and then disbelief,' says Gary Peterson, one of the assistant coaches with the Scottish team. 'They knew Scotland existed, but only as a beautiful country. So there was shock at the huge
15   impact the Scots had in the pool.'

Gary and I are talking at the Scottish National Open Age Group Championships in Glasgow's Tollcross Park Leisure Centre. It's the first major under-18 competition since the Commonwealth Games, and Gary has come back to Scotland with a splash. He hasn't even been home to Aberdeen yet from
20 Melbourne, but he's here coaching South Aberdeenshire swimming.

Screaming, laughing and cheers echo around the packed arena. 'Go Rachel! Go!' yells one parent in the stands, waving like a punter at the horse races.

Coaches, trainers and judges, dressed in surgical white, stalk the poolside, clipboards and stopwatches attached. Team mates stand at the top of each lane,
25 encouraging their friends towards their personal best and away from a humiliating last place. Queen's *Another One Bites the Dust* bellows from the speakers every time a Scottish age record is broken. It is played a lot today.

Trying to make out what someone is saying in conversation amid the hubbub is tough – like an aural kaleidoscope. But the smiles on faces, and
30 enthusiastic gestures tell their own story about the state of Scottish swimming.

But what does it cost to become a member of this new generation of swimmers? Speaking to aspiring Olympian Adrian O'Neill, quite a lot.

'It's a really hard sport,' says the fifteen-year old. 'You have to be really focused on it if you want to achieve anything. All your friends are having
35 parties and you just have to say "No, I've got to train". That's hard. But it's worthwhile, and it's fun.'

Like most swimmers Adrian gets up at 5 am to train for two hours in the pool before heading to school. Then it's a few more hours of swimming before hitting the sack. Staying up until 9 pm is seen as extravagant.
40 As if on cue, the commentator starts bellowing. Swimmers from Manchester and Middlesbrough who had been leading throughout the 400m individual medley start to tire. 'And it's Blaine Small from Glenrothes out in front!' screams the announcer. Seconds later Scotland has another victor in the pool. We could get used to this.

Questions

1 How does the author's word choice in the headline and sub-heading entertain the reader?

2 A

2 Explain how the examples given in paragraph one reinforce the points made in the opening sentence of the passage.

2 U/A

3   Comment on the effectiveness of any aspect of the structure of the first
    sentence in paragraph one.   **2 A**

4   How suitable do you find the author's choice of the word 'spark' in line 2?   **2 A**

5   Comment on the tone of 'but this is ancient history' (line 4).   **2 A**

6   Explain how the first sentence in paragraph two (lines 8–11) forms an
    effective link.   **2 A**

7   What is the effect of 'walking away with' rather than, say, 'winning' in
    line 11?   **2 A**

8   Explain how the Australians reacted to the success of Scotland's swimmers.   **2 U**

9   Comment on the effectiveness of 'Gary has come back to Scotland with
    a splash' (lines 18–19).   **2 A**

10 Re-read lines 21–22. Explain how the author uses word choice and
    imagery here to convey the atmosphere inside the leisure centre.   **3 A**

11 a) What impression does the writer give of the 'coaches, trainers and
        judges' (lines 23–24)?   **1 U**

    b) By referring to **two** examples, show how he uses word choice to
        create this effect.   **2 A**

12 What evidence is given to support the comment that swimming is
    'a really hard sport' (line 33)?   **2 U**

13 The writer's main purpose in this passage is to convince the reader of the
    success of Scottish swimmers.

    Identify any **two** techniques he uses and comment on how well you
    believe he has achieved his purpose.   **4 E**

TOTAL MARKS: 30

Taking a closer look . . .

Effective word choice

Often you will be asked to comment on why a particular choice of word or
phrase is effective, as in question 7 above.

To answer this type of question, you should consider:

- why the writer has chosen that word and not another one with a similar
  meaning

- what extra associations the chosen word brings to mind, over and above its
  basic 'dictionary' meaning – i.e. what are the **connotations** of the word?

For example

If we say 'I hammered at the door' rather than 'I knocked at the door', the choice of the word 'hammered' suggests that the knocking was done in a forceful, angry, impatient manner.

On the other hand, the connotations of 'knocking' are more neutral. The word doesn't reveal anything of the *manner* in which the action was carried out.

For practice

For written work or group discussion

Comment on the effectiveness of the underlined words in each of the following examples:

1 There's been the occasional, <u>glorious</u> spark in football, such as Celtic winning the European Cup in 1967. (The writer might have chosen to say 'bright'.)

2 100m Olympic champion Alan Wells won that title over a <u>quarter of a century ago</u>. (The writer might have chosen to say '25 years ago'.)

3 Scotland <u>ruled the pool</u> at the Commonwealth Games.

4 Queen's *Another One Bites the Dust* <u>bellows</u> from the speakers every time a Scottish age record is broken.

5 Staying up until 9 pm is seen as <u>extravagant.</u>

Chapter 5

'I'm Not Scared!'

In this passage, the novelist Julie Myerson thinks about why she enjoys horror films, while other people hate them.

1   Sunday lunch at my sister-in-law's. We're discussing a new horror film in which our 13-year-old, acting-mad, nephew Caspar landed a small role. Though everyone wants to see him in his first feature film, his mum won't see the film (too scary) and neither will his granny nor his uncle (my scaredy-cat husband).

5   Caspar's dad has seen it and says it's pretty frightening but 'not in a disturbing way'. My children and I are keen to see it – especially my 14-year-old, who is magnetically attracted to any 15 certificate. In his defence, he points out that this hasn't stopped Caspar himself seeing it.

    For years now, my husband and I have slugged it out on whether or not it's
10   good to be scared by art. I'm still cross that I never got to see *The Blair Witch Project* because he wouldn't come and I didn't (quite) dare go alone. So it's interesting to discover that, despite being the mother of a horror movie star, my husband's sister feels exactly the same. 'These things just stay with me,' she says, with a shudder. 'They haunt me.'

15   My husband's angle is that he gets nothing whatsoever from it, so why put himself through it? But that's the whole point, I say, to put yourself through it!

I don't like watching violence, but I find it both fun and useful to be frightened – spooked, terrified, scared witless! – by movies. And the reason they don't haunt me afterwards (not for long anyway) is that nothing that I

20   encounter is ever much worse than the dark material that already exists in my own head.

But then what does this say about me and my head? Do my husband and his sister have much sunnier minds than I do? Or is their dark stuff just as dark, except they won't go there? As a novelist, I know I write about the things that

25   frighten me – loss, fear, the raw black edges of life. Being allowed to do this makes me feel safe. Writing lets me peer over into that dark abyss of fear while knowing I can pull back at any time.

Speaking of fear, I remember a rare time when I was truly frightened and not in a harmless way. Researching a novel a few years ago, I thought I should

30   visit a Victorian prison. It did not look especially worrying when I arrived there one sunny weekday morning – even though I seemed to be the only visitor.

I paid my money and went in, obediently following the yellow-arrowed trail that led into a maze of dark tunnels and dungeons. After two minutes, I realised that a) I was utterly alone, b) it was abysmally dark, c) I could hear someone

35   crying, and d) I had no idea how much more there was. Yet e) if I turned back now, I could easily lose my way and no one would hear me screaming down there.

There was literally no going back. My heart was thumping and I could hear the pounding of my own blood as I made my way deeper and deeper into the

40   dank stone maze. When I finally emerged into the sunlight, I was shaking and sweaty.

I haven't thought about it in a long time, but, while writing this, I just googled it, only to discover that it's one of the most haunted sites in Britain. Now they tell me!

Questions

1   According to the writer, what was the main topic of conversation at Sunday lunch?   **1 U**

2   The author uses a chatty, informal style in the first paragraph. Pick out **two** expressions which are examples of this.   **2 A**

3 'Pretty frightening, but not in a disturbing way' (lines 5–6). In your own words, explain exactly what you think Caspar's father meant by this.   **2 U**

4 The writer says her 14-year-old is 'magnetically attracted' to any 15-certificate film (line 7). Explain how the writer's use of metaphor helps make her meaning clear in this statement.   **2 A**

5 a) Explain what the writer means by 'art' in line 10.   **1 U**

   b) Explain how the context helps you arrive at this meaning.   **1 U**

6 Read lines 11–14 'So it's interesting . . . haunt me.' In your own words, explain exactly why the writer's sister-in-law does not enjoy horror films.   **2 U**

7 Read lines 15–16 'My husband's angle . . . through it!' Explain in your own words why the writer's husband does not go to horror films.   **2 U**

8 Explain what you think the writer means in line 16 when she says 'the whole point [is] to put yourself through it'.   **2 U**

9 Read lines 17–21 'I don't like . . . own head.'

   a) Using quotation to support your answer, show how the writer uses word choice, sentence structure and punctuation to develop her idea of being frightened in the cinema.   **3 A**

   b) How does the phrase in parenthesis 'not for long anyway' (line 19) affect both the meaning and tone of the sentence in which it is used?   **2 U/A**

10 'Speaking of fear, I remember a rare time when I was truly frightened and not in a harmless way.' (lines 28–29)

   Show how this sentence acts as a link in the argument.   **2 A**

11 Read lines 38–41 'There was . . . sweaty'. Explain how the writer's word choice effectively conveys her feelings of fear in the Victorian prison.   **3 A**

12 When the writer looks up the Victorian prison on the Internet she discovers it is 'one of the most haunted sites in Britain' (line 43). Is there any evidence in the passage that she might agree with this view?   **1 U**

13 Explain how the writer's style effectively captures the reader's interest in the passage as a whole. Refer to at least two of: word choice; tone; use of parenthesis; colloquial language; sentence structure.   **4 E**

TOTAL MARKS: 30

Taking a closer look . . .

Context questions

Look again at question 5. You were asked to explain the meaning of the word 'art', by thinking about the context – how it is used in the passage.

'Art' usually means painting. But that would not make sense here. The meaning must have the wider sense of 'work of imagination' or 'visual creation'. Suggesting an appropriate meaning will gain 1 mark.

We know this because the writer refers to a film, *The Blair Witch Project*, as an example of 'art' which may frighten the viewer. Such an explanation will gain 1 mark.

For practice

Try the following examples. Even if you already know the meaning, think about how the context helps make it clear.

If you have no idea of the meaning, refer to a dictionary, and then attempt the second part of the question.

1. a) Explain what the writer means by 'sunnier' in line 23. (1)
   b) Explain how the context helps you arrive at this meaning. (1)

2. a) Explain what the writer means by 'abyss' in line 26. (1)
   b) Explain how the context helps you arrive at this meaning. (1)

3. a) Explain what the writer means by 'researching' in line 29. (1)
   b) Explain how the context helps you arrive at this meaning. (1)

4. a) Explain what the writer means by 'maze' in line 33. (1)
   b) Explain how the context helps you arrive at this meaning. (1)

Chapter 6

Flying Without Fear

In this passage Mark Stratton describes how he benefited from going on a course designed to help people overcome their fear of flying.

Extract

1   If you were offered a free first-class air-ticket to anywhere, with a five-star hotel
on arrival and £50,000 spending money, chances are you'd be delighted. Yet
psychologist David Landau's generous offer was being flatly refused. 'How
about £500,000?' he persisted, increasing his offer in front of an assembled
5   audience of nervous flyers. 'Still no,' replied Dawn. Bribery, it seemed, wasn't
going to get her airborne.

It's estimated that ten million people in Britain suffer from fear of flying.
For some, this represents a phobia that will ground sufferers; for most, it simply
means flying with heightened anxiety. Yet it can easily ruin a trip if you're
10   fretting about your return flights as soon as you arrive.

Despite flying over twenty times each year, I've never liked it. My big
problem is take-off. Palms sweat as soon as we taxi onto the runway and by lift-
off I'm gripping the armrests so tightly they could snap. As we ascend, I'm
acutely aware of the slightest variation in engine pitch as a nagging little voice
15   in my head whispers: 'Engine failure is imminent; we're all about to die.'

Fortunately, my wanderlust always overcomes my anxiety. And once we're cruising I really quite enjoy flying. Well, at least until the meals arrive. But, like many nervous flyers, I've also developed a rather irrational ritual as a coping strategy for take-off. I clutch a pendant (a carved leatherback turtle from Costa
20 Rica) in one hand and cross myself three times with the other – particularly illogical as I'm a self-professed atheist. Nevertheless, I subconsciously believe that this ritual will help keep us airborne.

It was time to seek some professional help.

Virgin Atlantic has been running Flying Without Fear courses since 1997,
25 helping over 10,000 people to jettison their fears. The day-long seminars lift-off from airports around the country.

What makes these confidence-building courses unique is that, after time in the classroom, participants put the theory to test on a short flight. Proceedings started with us dividing into small groups for a brainstorming session. We listed
30 what we disliked about flying: strange noises, turbulence, cabin claustrophobia, and so on. The course-trainers were truly up against it.

Enter current Virgin Airbus 340 pilots David Kistruck and Dom Riley. With a humorous repertoire of science and technical information, they explained just how safe modern jets are. They started with some physics, explaining how the
35 concept of 'lift' ensures aeroplanes can actually fly without engines just in case one or two drop off mid-flight. And they offered well-honed responses to floods of questions unleashed from the hall's nervy gathering. Yes, pilots undergo regular and rigorous training. Yes, aeroplanes are maintained thoroughly. Yes, there are multiple hydraulic systems in case one fails. No, the intercom 'bing
40 bongs' are not coded messages of doom. And wings wobble because if they were rigid 'it would be like driving a Reliant Robin down a cobbled street with no suspension.'

I found their presentation on the mechanical noises experienced during take-off particularly helpful. 'The first clunk is good,' said Captain Riley, 'as it
45 means eight tonnes of undercarriage have safely retracted.' Then, at 450m, a sudden throttling back of power (which always sends my pulse racing) is actually allowing the wing-flaps to straighten to increase aerodynamic efficiency.

The captains then headed straight into turbulence – the *bête noire* of all
50 nervous flyers. No commercial flight has ever been brought down by turbulence, they reassured. In fact, your main threat during turbulence, quipped Captain Kistruck, 'is somebody standing above you with a hot coffee.'

As departure time beckoned it fell upon psychoanalyst and Einstein-lookalike David Landau to relax our minds for take-off. 'Fear has two enemies,'

55 he began, 'knowledge and laughter.' Landau encouraged us to reduce pre-flight tension by laughing at the doom-laden negativity surrounding airports (words like 'terminal', 'departure lounge' and 'final destination' aren't too jolly, are they?). We were told we suffer from fear, not phobias, which can be overcome. A phobic wouldn't have made it to Heathrow, he claimed. Finally, we were

60 lulled into a session of meditative deep breathing to banish the 'ball of fear' from the pit of our stomachs.

Eventually the coaches arrive to take us to Terminal (ha-ha-ha!) One. For one lady, it was all too much – she ejected before we even began to taxi. Captain Kistruck provided a running commentary as we set off for a half-hour spin

65 around north London. There were no screams on take-off, although some of my fellow flyers exhibited less colour than an in-flight salad. After circling in cloudless skies, we returned to earth. Applause broke out on touchdown – like landing in Latin America after a transatlantic flight.

I'll wait for my next 'solo' flight before deciding if I've truly benefited. But

70 the omens look good – behind me I heard an excited voice comment: 'Shame there wasn't a little more turbulence.' It was Dawn.

Questions

1 Quote the sentence from lines 1–6 that best sums up the point the author is making in paragraph one. **1 U**

2 Basing your answer on paragraph two (lines 7–10), explain in your own words **two** possible effects that fear of flying can have on passengers. **2 U**

3 a) Why is it surprising that the writer suffers from a fear of flying? **1 U**

b) Explain **two** ways in which he conveys the effects of this fear in paragraph three (lines 11–15). **2 A**

4 What does the author mean when he says 'my wanderlust always overcomes my anxiety' (line 16)? **2 U**

5 Explain how the author makes fun of his fear in the rest of paragraph four (lines 16–22). **2 A**

6 Show how the sentence 'It was time to seek some professional help' (line 23) provides a link between the previous paragraph and the one that follows. **2 A**

7 a) 'The day-long seminars lift-off from airports around the country' (lines 25–26). Why is 'lift-off' an effective choice of word here? **2 A/E**

  b) From elsewhere in the passage, quote another phrase or sentence which is used to achieve a similar effect. **1 A**

8 'With a humorous repertoire of science and technical information, [the pilots] explained just how safe modern jets are' (lines 32–34).

  a) In your own words, give **one** example of how a technical explanation was given to reassure the audience. **2 U**

  b) Quote one example of humour used by the pilots and explain why you found this effective. **3 U/A**

9 Explain how successful you find the image or metaphor 'floods of questions' (lines 36–37). **2 A**

10 Comment on any aspect of the sentence structure used in paragraph eight (lines 36–42) which you consider to be particularly effective. **2 A**

11 Suggest **one** reason why the passengers applauded when the plane touched down. **2 U**

12 Look again at paragraph 11 (lines 53–61). Explain the difference between 'fear' and 'phobia'. **2 U**

13 How successful do you find the last paragraph as a conclusion to the passage as a whole? **2 E**

TOTAL MARKS: **30**

Taking a closer look . . .

Opening paragraphs

Newspaper and magazine articles such as 'Flying Without Fear' need an opening that will arouse the reader's interest .

Here are a few of the methods that writers use to achieve these aims:

- a humorous comment
- an anecdote (a story to illustrate a point)
- a personal experience
- a surprising fact or statistics
- a question to make the reader think
- a summary of the main ideas to be examined in detail in the rest of the passage.

For practice

'Flying Without Fear' originally appeared as an article in the travel magazine *Wanderlust*. Here are some more extracts from the magazine, taken from the opening paragraphs of other articles.

In pairs or groups, discuss how effective each paragraph is as an introduction. What methods does the writer use to grab the reader's attention? Are there any clues about what the rest of the article is going to discuss?

How to be a flight attendant

Until someone invents a 'beam me up' type transporter, you're unlikely to knock off work and find yourself in a different country to the one you started in. Unless, that is, your day's work happens to involve manning a commercial airline. The idea that life as a flight attendant is one long glamorous jetset might explain the job's appeal – but, of course, the image only portrays a tiny part of the reality.

The Great Wall of China

The Great Wall of China, a fortified line stretching 4,000km across deserts, mountains and grasslands, is a true Wonder – and a costly military mistake. But no matter that it never worked; today it's irresistibly romantic, and deservedly China's top sight.

Just truckin': a five week overland trip in Africa

Apart from a bout of malaria, a box-jellyfish attack, several baboon raids, a lost passport and a mauling by a lion, the trip went off with surprisingly few mishaps. Fair enough, our departure from Nairobi had hardly been the death-or-glory stuff of the 1887 Count Teleki expedition. Far from heading into uncharted territory in a land of potentially murderous tribes, we were following the well-trodden overland trail through many of the most famous sights in East Africa. We were almost as well equipped as the Count – minus the boxes of ammunition and cases of 'medicinal' Scotch – but in place of a team of 450 native porters we had loaded all our provisions into a huge, wallowing yellow truck known affectionately as 'The Whale'.

Chapter 7

Taking the Train to Windsor

In his best-selling book *Notes From a Small Island*, the American writer Bill Bryson describes a round-Britain tour. In this passage he encounters a crowd of rugby fans on a train.

Extract

1 When I revealed that I was planning to travel around Britain by public transport, everyone I saw said, 'Gosh, you're brave!' but it never occurred to me to go any other way. Driving in Britain is such a dreary experience these days. There are far too many cars on the road, nearly double what there were when I first came

5 here, and in those days people didn't actually drive their cars. They just parked them in the driveway and buffed them up once every week, or so. About twice a year they would 'get the car out' – those were the words they used, like that in itself was a big operation – and pootle off to visit relatives or have a trip to someplace like Eastbourne, and that was about it, apart from the buffing.

10   Now everyone drives everywhere for everything, which I don't understand because there isn't a single feature of driving in Britain that has even the tiniest measure of enjoyment in it. Just consider the average multi-storey car park. You drive around for ages, and then spend a small eternity shunting into a space that

is exactly two inches wider than the average car. Then, because you are parked
15 next to a pillar, you have to climb over the seats and end up squeezing out of
the passenger door, in the process transferring all the dirt from the side of your
car to the back of your smart new jacket from Marks & Spencer. Then you go
hunting for some distant pay-and-display machine, which doesn't give change,
and wait on an old guy who likes to read all the instructions on the machine
20 before committing himself and then tries to insert his money through the ticket
slot and maintenance keyhole. Eventually you acquire a ticket and trek back to
your car where your wife greets you with a 'Where have you been?'

Ignoring her, you squeeze past the pillar, collecting a matching set of dust
for the front of your jacket, discover that you can't reach the windscreen as the
25 door only opens three inches, so you just sort of throw the ticket at the
dashboard (it flutters to the floor) and squeeze back out where your wife sees
what a scruff you've turned into after she spent all that time dressing you and
beats the dust from you with paddled hands while saying, 'Honestly, I can't take
you *anywhere.*'

30 And that's just the beginning. Arguing quietly, you have to find your way
out of this dank hellhole via an unmarked door leading to a curious chamber
that seems to be a composite of dungeon and urinal, or else wait two hours for
the world's most abused and unreliable looking lift, which will only take two
people and already has two people in it – a man whose wife is beating dust from
35 his new Marks & Spencer jacket and berating him in clucking tones.

And the remarkable thing is that everything about this process is
intentionally – mark this, intentionally – designed to flood your life with
unhappiness. From the tiny parking bays that can only be got into by
manoeuvring your car through a forty-six point turn (why can't the spaces be
40 angled, for crying out loud?) to the careful placing of pillars where they will
cause maximum obstruction, to the ramps that are so dark and narrow and badly
angled that you always bump the kerb, to the remote, wilfully unhelpful ticket
machines (you can't tell me that a machine that can recognize and reject any
foreign coin ever produced couldn't make change if it wanted to) – all of this is
45 designed to make this the most dispiriting experience of your adult life.

And that's just one tiny part of the driving experience. There are all the
other manifold annoyances of motoring, like white van drivers who pull out in
front of you on motorways, 8-mile-long contraflow systems erected so that
some guys on a crane can change a light bulb, traffic lights on busy roundabouts
50 that never let you advance more than 20 feet at a time, motorway service areas
where you have to pay £9.80 for a mini-pot of coffee and a jacket potato with a
sneeze of cheddar in it, morons with caravans who pull out of side-roads just

as you approach, and other challenges to your patience and sanity nearly beyond endurance. Motorized vehicles are ugly and dirty and they bring out the
55   worst in people. They clutter every kerbside, turn ancient market squares into disorderly jumbles of metal, spawn petrol stations, Kwik-fit centres and other dispiriting blights. They are horrible and awful and I wanted nothing to do with them on this trip. And besides, my wife wouldn't let me have the car.

      Thus it was that I found myself late on a grey Saturday afternoon, on an
60   exceptionally long and empty train bound for Windsor. I sat high on the seat in an empty carriage, and in fading daylight watched as the train slid past office blocks and out into the forests of council flats and snaking terrace houses of Vauxhall and Clapham. At Twickenham, I discovered why the train was so long and was so empty. The platform was jammed solid with men and boys in warm
65   clothes and scarves carrying glossy programmes and little bags with tea flasks peeping out: obviously a rugby crowd from the Twickenham grounds.

      They boarded with patience and without pushing, and said sorry when they bumped or inadvertently impinged on someone else's space. I admired this instinctive consideration for others, and was struck by what a regular thing that
70   is in Britain and how little it is noticed. Nearly everyone rode all the way to Windsor – I presume there must be some sort of parking arrangement there; Windsor can't provide that many rugby fans – and formed a patient crush at the ticket barrier. An Asian man collected tickets in fast motion and said thank you to every person who passed. He didn't have time to examine the tickets – you
75   could have handed him a cornflakes box top – but he did manage to find a vigorous salute for all, and they in turn thanked him for relieving them of their tickets and letting them pass. It was a little miracle of orderliness and goodwill. Anywhere else there'd have been someone on a box barking at people to form a line and not to push.

Questions

1 Read the first two sentences 'When I revealed . . . these days.' In your own words, explain

   a) how people reacted when the writer said he was travelling round Britain by public transport   **1 U**

   b) why he chose to go by public transport.   **1 U**

2 Read lines 5–9. In your own words explain how, according to the writer, people in the past used their cars.   **2 U**

3 'There isn't a single feature of driving in Britain that has even the tiniest measure of enjoyment in it.' (lines 11–12) Identify **one** technique the writer uses in this sentence, and explain its effect.   **2 A**

4 Look again at lines 12–22 where Bryson describes the difficulties of using a multi-storey car park. Show how he uses word choice and sentence structure effectively to express these difficulties.   **4 A**

5 Comment on the writer's use of the phrase 'arguing quietly' in line 30.   **2 A**

6 Show how the context helps you arrive at the meaning of 'berating' (line 35).   **2 U**

7 Show how the sentence 'And that's just one tiny part of the driving experience' (line 46) acts as a link in the argument.   **2 A**

8 Read again the list of 'annoyances' in lines 46–54. In your own words, explain why any **two** of these could be an 'annoyance' to the motorist.   **2 U**

9 'And besides, my wife wouldn't let me have the car.' (line 58) Explain how the meaning of this sentence and its position in the paragraph has a humorous effect.   **2 A**

10 Read again lines 60–63 'I sat high on the seat . . . Clapham.' Referring to any **one** example, show how the writer has used imagery effectively to describe what he sees from the train.   **2 A**

11 Look again at lines 67–79. In your own words, list **four** of the ways in which people impressed the writer with their good manners.   **4 U**

12 The writer, Bill Bryson, always uses a highly personal style in his travel writing. With close discussion of at least **two** examples, explain how he puts over a sense of his own personality effectively in this passage.   **4 E**

TOTAL MARKS: **30**

Taking a closer look ...

Summary

A type of 'Understanding' question which you will frequently meet in Close Reading tests is the summary. A summary question may be worth quite a lot of marks and so it is important to tackle it correctly.

Points to remember in summary questions:

- Always use your own words as far as possible.
- Be as brief as possible in expressing the ideas.
- Use bullet points rather than a paragraph format to show you have given the required number of ideas in your answer.
- There is no need to write in sentences – note form will do. (Your writing skills are not tested in Close Reading.)

And finally,

- Make sure you complete the question!

Summary questions worth several marks may appear near the end of a question paper. They generally offer an easy way to pick up marks, but you will only gain this advantage if you manage your time properly and get the question finished.

Question 11 on the previous page is a typical summary question. You are asked to express **four** ideas from the passage in the form of a list:

> Look again at lines 67–79. In your own words, list **four** of the ways in which people impressed the writer with their good manners.   **4 U**

Possible answers might have included the following:

- The rugby fans waited patiently to get on the train.
- They did not push one another as they got on.
- They apologised if they knocked into someone or got too close.
- They waited patiently in line at Windsor to show their tickets.
- The ticket collector thanked each one of the fans politely.
- The rugby fans thanked the ticket collector for checking their tickets.
- The ticket collector did not treat the fans disrespectfully by shouting or giving orders.

Any four of the above points given in this form would have gained full marks for the question.

Would it be a good idea to give more than four points to make sure of gaining full marks?

There is really no need to do this, as the marker can only give you a maximum of 4 marks! However, if you are unsure that you have made two separate points (for example, in the case of the first two points about how the fans boarded the train) it would do no harm to add a fifth. But only do this if you know you have plenty of time to complete the rest of the test.

For practice

Try the following additional summary questions, both of which are based on part of the Bill Bryson passage. Provide answers in the form of bullet points.

Read lines 12–45 'Just consider . . . adult life.'

1 In your own words, list **five** separate design faults which the writer sees in the typical multi-storey car park.

2 In your own words, list **three** drawbacks which the writer mentions concerning the system of payment in the multi-storey car parks.

Chapter 8

Doctor, Doctor, I Keep Catching New Medical Shows

There are fourteen doctor dramas on TV right now. So why aren't we sick of them yet, asks Stephen Armstrong?

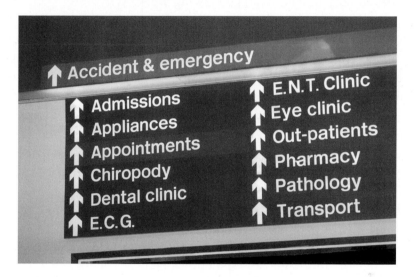

Extract

1 Let's play spot the plot. Which of the following actually happened? A nurse enjoys the intensity and drama of the casualty unit, so deliberately poisons patients for a thrill. A doctor has a political point to make, so allows certain patients to die in the operating theatre. A manual worker is bored with life on
5 the railways, so gives it up to become a doctor.

Okay, it's a cheat. They're all true. One of them, however, became the basis for *Vital Signs*, Tamzin Outhwaite's ITV drama. Outhwaite plays Rhoda Bradley, a supermarket assistant with three children who decides to secure some personal growth by, you know, becoming a doctor. It's just that her family wishes she'd
10 spend less time saving lives and more time microwaving the oven chips.

There have, of course, been medical dramas pretty much from the birth of commercial television. In this country, *Emergency Ward 10* debuted on ITV in 1957, although in those innocent days, actual medical nitty-gritty was considered too ghastly to feature prominently (Ward 10 was allowed a maximum of five
15 patient deaths per year).

Extract continued

Since then, there has been a steady trickle: *Angels*, *St Elsewhere*, *Casualty*, *Quincy*, *Chicago Hope* . . . you know the score. In television, they are called precinct drama, shorthand for series based around a particular work-related location and so named because US cop shows kicked off the genre. Over time,
20   we have watched the comings and goings of policemen, lawyers, city dealers, forensic teams and journalists, but for today's viewers there's only one precinct that counts: medicine. It's currently possible to absorb almost 24 hours of doctor-related telly in your average viewing week. Why?

In dramatic terms, the advantage of a medical setting is clear. 'It's far easier
25   for people to relate to the human-interest element in a medical drama than in a legal drama simply because they come across them every day,' says John Forte, the creator of *Vital Signs*.

It also helps that you can crowbar almost any event into a hospital room. 'There's almost nowhere other than a hospital where you can find all human life
30   under just one roof. You've got ordinary members of the public, office staff, medics, car-park attendants – we knew you could take a camera down the corridor of a hospital and find anything going on behind any of the doors,' explains Victoria Pile, the show's producer.

Perhaps that is why these shows proliferate: they can absorb and exude the
35   attributes of almost every other genre.

With the new breed of shows, however, there are additional symptoms. For one thing, doctors misdiagnose – sometimes fatally. The idea that medical staff are in some way heroic – which was true even of the layabout crew of *M*A*S*H* – is gradually slipping away. Sonia Livingstone, professor of social
40   psychology at the London School of Economics, says that 'there has always been a fascination with what goes on behind doctors' doors. That goes back as far as *Dr Finlay's Casebook*. The recent crop of shows, however, sees medical experts challenged. A few years ago, doctors and nurses were TV shorthand for trustworthy, well-intentioned people.'
45   Today, it seems, we're seeing the collapse of the doctor as saintly saviour.

Questions

1   Comment on the effectiveness of the headline used at the top of this
    article.   2 A

2 Look again at lines 6–10.

  a) What is the tone of 'Okay, it's a cheat'? **1 A**

  b) Quote another expression from this paragraph which helps to establish a similar tone. **1 A**

3 'It's just that her family wishes she'd spend less time saving lives and more time microwaving the oven chips.' (lines 9–10)

  a) In your own words, explain the attitude of the character's family to her desire to become a doctor. **2 U**

  b) Comment on how the structure of the above sentence helps to make this attitude clear. **2 A**

4 In your own words, explain how the 1950s TV series *Emergency Ward 10* was different from more recent hospital dramas. **2 U**

5 Look again at lines 16–17. Comment on any **two** techniques used in this sentence which help to convey the author's opinion of the large number of hospital dramas that have been made for television. **3 A**

6 In your own words, explain what is meant by the expression 'precinct drama' (line 18). **2 U**

7 Look again at lines 24–33. Explain in your own words the two advantages of using a hospital setting for a drama series. **4 U**

8 Comment on the effectiveness of the choice of the word 'crowbar' in line 28. **2 A**

9 Explain how the sentence 'With the new breed of shows, however, there are additional symptoms' (line 36) performs a linking function. **2 A**

10 Look again at lines 36–44.

  a) What view of medical staff did older TV programmes present? **1 U**

  b) Quote **two** adjectives that describe how doctors and nurses were viewed in these programmes. **1 A**

  c) Give one example of how medical staff are portrayed differently today. **1 U**

11 How far do you consider the final sentence to be an effective conclusion to this passage? **2 E**

12 What do you think the writer's main purpose is in this article? By referring to points made or techniques used, comment on how successful you think he has been in achieving his purpose. **2 E**

TOTAL MARKS: 30

Taking a closer look ...

Structuring an argument

An article like this needs to have a **structure**. The writer doesn't simply list points – he links them together.

Here are some of the methods he uses to make his sentences and paragraphs flow:

- In paragraph one (line 1) there is a question:

Which of the following actually happened?

This leads to three choices being stated, followed by an answer.

- Many paragraphs begin with a **topic sentence** – that is, a sentence that states the main point which is developed in more detail in the rest of the paragraph.

Paragraph five (line 24) begins:

In dramatic terms, the advantage of a medical setting is clear.

This is a general statement which is backed up in the rest of the paragraph by evidence, in this case a quotation from someone involved in the production of medical dramas for television.

- **Linking words and phrases** are used to lead from one point into the next, particularly at the start of paragraphs:

Since then (paragraph four)   –   uses a time link
It also helps (paragraph six)   –   'also' gives a sense of progression
However (paragraph eight)   –   creates a contrast or objection

For practice

Read the following short passages and discuss how the writers have given them a structure by using a variety of linking methods.

---

a)

1   **Slang and social identity**
How do social groups create their own identity? The main way is by developing their own style of language. When people learn to use the slang words that are in fashion then they are accepted as part of the group. But slang is something

5   that keeps evolving: words that were popular one year might be out-of-date the next, and anybody who doesn't keep up with the latest trends won't be accepted as part of the group.

However, one of the biggest influences on the way that language develops today is the media. Young people in particular are quick to pick up and use words they hear in television programmes. As a result, teenagers on both sides of the Atlantic, while they may speak with different accents, will recognise and use many similar slang expressions.

b)

Who are you looking at?

All people, whatever their age, are attracted by looks. That's why celebs like David Beckham, Jennifer Lopez and Brad Pitt are so widely admired.

If you're not gorgeous, though, don't despair. People don't always go for the best lookers. Beyond the initial attraction, personality is more important. Some people act like a magnet whatever their looks. They've got what's called charisma – a peculiar mixture of charm and personality. Take Sir Bob Geldof – he's no oil painting but he's got charisma, which means that people will always pay him attention. Furthermore, charismatic people attract others with their enthusiasm and energy, not the size of their eyes or the shape of their chin.

Body language says a great deal about your behaviour. Body language is all about the look on your face, the way you speak, and the signals you send by how you stand and move.

Take eye contact, for example. If you don't look at someone when you are introduced, it looks as if you are shy, aloof or have something to hide. But if you stare, that seems threatening and hostile.

The importance of body language is confirmed by the experts. 'If someone likes you, you will notice an increase in eye contact,' says body language and Big Brother expert Judi James. 'They will hold your gaze for a second or two longer than usual. Then they will keep glancing back to check your expression to see how you are reacting to them.'

Chapter 9

God Save the Queen

In this article, Charles Moore reflects on what it must be like to be the Queen.

Extract

1   Have you noticed that modern Britain is the most matriarchal society in the history of the world? The four most famous figures in the public service since the war have been women – the Queen Mother; the Queen; Diana, Princess of Wales; and Margaret Thatcher. Since the death of Winston Churchill more than
5   40 years ago, no British man has come near any of these four in the attention he can command.

     I cannot say what the effect of this curious fact has been on women, but, as a man, I feel very grateful. It has added interest, surprise and mystery to what would otherwise have been a flat landscape of men in suits.

10   Of the four, the Queen is the hardest to understand. This is partly because most of her subjects, including me, have nothing to compare her with. She came to the throne before I was born. You have to be 60 to remember anything else. As a result, the Queen has been less considered, less examined than the other three above. Questions such as 'What does she feel?' or 'How good is she at her
15   job?' seem somehow beside the point. She just is. She reigns.

In thinking about the Queen, I am conscious that I am probably doing something that would displease her. Can there ever have been anyone in public life with less desire to show off, bare her soul, win people's hearts or explain herself in any way? She no more wants to do such things than to be

20   photographed in the bath.

It is said that when the Queen sits for a portrait, she has never been known to pass comment on its portrayal of herself. She appears not to be interested in herself and she makes no assumption that anyone else will be.

To some people, such behaviour is almost inhuman. The Queen must be

25   terribly dull, they say, not to want to engage with her endlessly ready audience, or terribly cold, or terribly unhappy. And one does occasionally get the impression from the set of her jaw that the Queen is not particularly enjoying the latest display of mime in the rain or exhibition of old photographs of the Biggleswade Rotary Club that she is being subjected to.

30   But it seems much more likely that the Queen's methods are the result of a choice, carefully considered, early made and faithfully adhered to. In her famous broadcast from Cape Town, 59 years ago, Princess Elizabeth made a promise that 'the whole of my life, whether it be long or short' would be dedicated to the service of her country. Surely the Queen's life is an example,

35   perhaps the most astonishing in our history, of what it means to make a promise, and to keep it.

The promise directs everything. What is mere boredom beside it? I read or heard that the Queen has met, individually, three million people in her life. The very thought of boredom must be excluded from the mind to endure such a

40   thing.

So must exaggeration, over-demonstrativeness. At the time of her Golden Jubilee, a courtier told the story of how once, faced with the draft of a speech which said, 'I am very glad to be in Birmingham', the Queen crossed out the word 'very'. This is the exact opposite of the politician's instinct which would

45   be to wow Birmingham.

Her promise forbids the Queen to have views (one reason, no doubt, why she seems to find Prince Charles' interventions so irritating), since views detract from equal service to all. She must not have favourites, she must not abdicate, she must not show strong feelings. She must not get drunk or wear old clothes

50   or take a weekend break on a whim or do anything, ever, just because she feels like it. She must even put her duties as mother behind those as a sovereign. She must be like the face on the postage stamp and the coin – always there, always the same, always royal.

Questions

1. Explain **one** way in which the writer captures the attention of the reader in the opening sentence of the passage.

   1 A

2. a) Explain how the ideas of the second sentence (lines 2–4) help you arrive at the meaning of 'matriarchal' in line 1.

   2 U

   b) Show how the author's use of punctuation in the second sentence of the passage helps put over his ideas clearly.

   2 A

3. Show how the first sentence in paragraph two ('I cannot say . . . grateful') acts as a link in the argument at this point.

   2 U/A

4. 'It has added interest, surprise and mystery to what would otherwise have been a flat landscape of men in suits.' (lines 8–9)

   a) In your own words, explain clearly how the 'flat landscape' image used by the writer helps you appreciate his meaning.

   2 A

   b) In your own words, explain clearly what the writer means by 'interest, surprise and mystery'.

   3 U

5. 'She just is. She reigns'. (line 15) Explain how the sentence structure here is effective as a conclusion to paragraph three.

   2 A/E

6. 'She no more wants to do such things than to be photographed in the bath.' (lines 19–20) Explain how the author uses comparison effectively in this sentence.

   2A/E

7. a) Explain in your own words what the author means when he says that you can tell 'from the set of her jaw' (line 27) that the Queen is not enjoying herself.

   1 U

   b) 'mime in the rain or exhibition of old photographs of the Biggleswade Rotary Club.' (lines 28–29) Referring to tone and/or word choice, comment on the author's choice of examples of the Queen's engagements.

   2 A

8. 'The very thought of boredom must be excluded from the mind to endure such a thing'. (lines 38–40) Explain in your own words what the author means by this.

   2 U

9. a) Read the last two paragraphs (lines 41–53). Suggest **two** reasons why the Queen may have asked for the word 'very' to be crossed out, according to the courtier's story in lines 41–44.

   2 U

   b) In lines 48–51, the writer lists things which the Queen must not do. In your own words, summarise **four** of the points the writer makes.

   4 U

57

c) Which single word in the last paragraph suggests that the most difficult thing for the Queen may be to put her duties as a mother behind her duties to the state? **1 U**

d) Comment on the sentence structure and ideas the writer uses in the last sentence of the passage, showing how it provides an effective conclusion to the article as a whole. **2 A/E**

TOTAL MARKS: 30

Taking a closer look ...

Link questions

In question 3, you were asked to 'show how the first sentence in paragraph two acts as a link in the argument at this point'.

The sentence was:

I cannot say what the effect of this curious fact has been on women, but, as a man, I feel very grateful.

Good writers make their arguments flow by leading the reader gently from one idea to the next. They do this by using linking sentences which refer both to the idea they have just been discussing, and also to the next idea to be dealt with.

Usually, the sentence will come at the start of a paragraph, but occasionally it will come at the end, or even in the middle of a paragraph which deals with more than one topic.

In a question like the one above, your task is to analyse exactly how this process works in the selected sentence. Your answer should **quote** the word or words which refer to the previous topic, explaining **in your own words** what that topic was, and it should then **quote** the word (or words) referring to the new topic, saying in your own words what it is.

A good answer to question 3 would read:

> The phrase 'this curious fact' refers back to his point in the previous paragraph that, surprisingly, the four most world-famous British people recently have all been women. The idea 'I feel very grateful' is expanded in the next part of the paragraph where he explains why he is happy about this 'curious fact'.

The answer would gain 1 mark for the first quotation and correct summing up of the topic and 1 mark for the second quotation and summary. Remember that your answer to a link question should always contain four elements.

For practice

This writer uses link sentences throughout his article to lead his reader easily from one topic to the next. Using the method that has just been explained, and including four elements in each answer, show how each of the following sentences acts as a link in the argument.

1 'Of the four, the Queen is the hardest to understand.' (line 10)

2 'In thinking about the Queen, I am conscious that I am probably doing something that would displease her.' (lines 16–17)

3 'To some people, such behaviour is almost inhuman.' (line 24)

4 'But it seems much more likely that the Queen's methods are the result of a choice, carefully considered, early made and faithfully adhered to.' (lines 30–31)

5 'The promise directs everything.' (line 37)

Chapter 10

On the Orient Express

Crime writer Agatha Christie set one of her murder mysteries on the Orient Express, a train which people associate with the glamour and romance of the 1930s when the book was written. In this article, Victoria Coren describes her experience on the Orient Express of today.

Extract

1   Bedtime on the Orient Express. We stood in the corridor while a hatchet-faced
Austrian woman yanked our bunk-beds into place – there wasn't room in the
carriage for all three of us. Barking the news that she would be waking us at
7 a.m. with a cup of instant coffee and a piece of cheese, the woman departed
5   and we retired for the night.

'Bunk-beds?' you may be thinking. Small carriage? Instant coffee? This
can't be the *real* Orient Express! Oh, but it is. This is a very real Orient Express
indeed. And it's a lot cheaper than the famous one. In search of a long weekend
in Vienna, there seemed no more enchanting way for my friend and me to get
10   there.

The original Orient Express service was launched in 1863. Luxury carriages
ran the route from Paris to Giugiu (on the Danube in Romania) via Strasbourg,

Vienna, Budapest and Bucharest. In 1921, the route was extended to Istanbul, and the trains carried socialites, aristocrats, flappers[1], artists and spies on
15   glamorous journeys across Europe. They dined in the restaurant car, guzzled fine wines, and crept between each other's lavishly-appointed compartments. In 1934, Agatha Christie sent Hercule Poirot on just such a journey in her novel *Murder On The Orient Express.*

World War II brought an end to all this glorious rattling around. There was
20   a rise in air travel which was quicker and cheaper and eventually the whole operation ground to a halt in 1977. The name was relaunched in 1982, when the Venice Simplon-Orient-Express took its maiden voyage between London and Venice. This is the luxury train that most people think of when they hear the name. But the original 'Orient Express' was a line, not a train. In fact, if you
25   take an ordinary train today between Paris and Vienna, you are still, officially, 'taking the Orient Express'. Which is what we did.

Admittedly I would have loved to take the Venice Simplon-Orient-Express, with its on-board boutique and baby grand piano in the bar, but at around £1,700 per person for a four-night one-way journey, we couldn't afford it. So
30   we chose this excellent way of buying into the romance for a fraction of the cost.

When we arrived at the Gare de l'Est in Paris (easily accessible nowadays, of course, with the clean and efficient Eurostar whistling directly into Paris from Kent), we found the words 'Orient Express' pinned up in the window of
35   the relevant SNCF[2] train. In other respects, the train wasn't impressive. It needed a clean on the outside. There was no restaurant car, only 'Helga' with a platter of cold meats and cheeses, plus the picnic we had picked up in Paris. There was no first class section, only a choice between a private sleeping car (which we took: two chairs and a small table, with bunk-beds which folded
40   down when we were ready for bed); sharing a six bed compartment; or reclining seats in an ordinary carriage.

But we loved it. Ours was no luxury bedroom, but it had its own rough charm – not to mention the magic of rattling across international borders overnight, following the same route that all those spies and socialites had taken
45   before us. I haven't slept in a bunk-bed since I was seven, and clambering up into it took 25 years off me. For one night only, it was cosily appealing. Naturally, I took a copy of *Murder On The Orient Express* to read on the train. I smiled wryly at the descriptions of airy dining-cars and fresh coffee.

[1] flappers: fashionable young women of the 1920s and 1930s
[2] SNCF: French national railways (Société Nationale des Chemins de Fer)

50   We left Paris around 5 p.m. and (having been woken by Helga with the promised cheese, and a chance to see sunrise over Austria) slid into Vienna at 8.30 a.m. The weekend in Vienna included a day trip to Baden, a beautiful little cobbled spa town. The air smelt of sulphur and spicy fruit punch, but I neatly avoided both by ducking into the glittering casino for which Baden is also famous. It went terribly well - in fact, I won nearly enough for a trip on the

55   expensive Orient Express.

But reunited with the cut-price Orient Express at the end of the holiday, we were rather delighted to see our little compartment again. Good old bunk-beds. Terrifying old Helga. Homeward, we trundled: carriages shook, cheese was consumed, and (best of all) nobody got murdered.

Questions

1 a)   Quote **two** words or expressions from paragraph one which illustrate the manner of the woman attendant on the train.   **2 A**

   b)   Explain clearly what each of your examples conveys about the woman's manner.   **4 U/A**

2 Read again lines 1–5. In your own words, describe any **one** aspect of the accommodation or catering on the Orient Express and how it contrasts with the pampering and luxury which travellers might expect.   **2 U**

3 Explain how the writer produces an ironic tone in lines 6–10 to express disbelief at aspects of the new Orient Express. (You might mention sentence structure, punctuation, use of italics etc.)   **2 A**

4 In lines 11–13, the author lists many places on the route of the first Orient Express. Suggest a reason why she mentions these particular places.   **1 A**

5 a)   In lines 14–18 the author describes the glamorous travellers on the earliest version of the Orient Express. Identify **one** word which seems inappropriate in describing them.   **1 A**

   b)   Explain why this word seems inappropriate in this context.   **2 A**

6 Explain in your own words the main reason why the Orient Express ceased to run in 1977.   **1 U**

7 Comment on any one of the images used by the author in lines 19–23 and explain why it is effective.   **2 A**

8 Explain how, according to lines 24–26, the writer and her friend were 'officially' taking the Orient Express. **2 U**

9 Read lines 27–48.

   a) Explain **two** ways in which the sentence 'But we loved it' is effective at this point in the passage. **2 A/E**

   b) Explain in your own words why the author and her friend 'loved' the journey, despite the lack of luxury on the train. **2 U**

10 a) Suggest a reason why the writer took *Murder On The Orient Express* with her to read on the train. **1 U**

    b) Explain how the context helps you understand the meaning of the word 'wryly' in line 48. **2 U**

11 Using examples to illustrate your answer, explain how the writer creates an effective conclusion in the final paragraph. In your answer, you should refer to at least **two** of the following: ideas; word choice; tone; sentence structure. **4 E**

TOTAL MARKS: **30**

Taking a closer look …

Sentence structure

Some questions in Close Reading tests will ask you to talk about sentence structure. It is essential that you are able to recognise the different techniques and patterns used by writers so that you can describe them and comment on their effect.

In the passage on the Orient Express, Victoria Coren uses a wide variety of structures.

Here are three techniques she has used more than once:

- **Minor sentences** – sentences without verbs or without a principal clause, e.g. 'Bedtime on the Orient Express' (line 1).

- **Rhetorical questions** – questions that create a particular tone, but do not expect an answer, e.g. 'Bunk-beds?' (line 6).

- **Parenthesis** – words added in brackets which either give more detail or provide a comment, e.g. '(on the Danube in Romania)' (line 12).

For practice (1)

In each of the following examples, (a) identify which of these three techniques has been used and (b) try to explain the effect of the technique. In the case of parenthesis, decide whether the writer is **adding detail** or **making a comment** in the additional words. (Occasionally you may find more than one technique in a single example.)

a) 'Small carriage? Instant coffee?' (line 6)

b) 'Which is what we did.' (line 26)

c) 'When we arrived at the Gare de l'Est in Paris (easily accessible nowadays, of course, with the clean and efficient Eurostar whistling directly into Paris from Kent), we found the words "Orient Express" pinned up in the window of the relevant SNCF train.' (lines 32–35)

d) 'We left Paris around 5 p.m. and (having been woken by Helga with the promised cheese, and a chance to see sunrise over Austria) slid into Vienna at 8.30 a.m.' (lines 49–51)

e) 'Terrifying old Helga.' (line 58)

f) '. . . and (best of all) nobody got murdered.' (line 59)

Listing and climax

Another technique of sentence structure used frequently by Victoria Coren in the Orient Express article is listing. Listing may be used in one of two ways.

A list may be simply three or more items of equal importance, or it may consist of three or more items gradually rising in significance to a **climax** if the last one is the most important, or descending to an **anticlimax**, if the last item is less important than the others. If you notice a list, always think about whether it may form a climax or anticlimax.

For practice (2)

In the following examples, decide whether the writer is using a simple list (with items of similar importance) or whether there is a progression in importance towards a climax or anticlimax. Justify your answer each time.

a) 'via Strasbourg, Vienna, Budapest and Bucharest.' (lines 12–13)

b) 'the trains carried socialites, aristocrats, flappers, artists and spies' (line 14)

c) 'They dined in the restaurant car, guzzled fine wines, and crept between each other's lavishly-appointed compartments.' (lines 15–16)

d) 'two chairs and a small table, with bunk-beds which folded down' (lines 39–40)

e) 'carriages shook, cheese was consumed, and (best of all) nobody got murdered.' (lines 58–59)

Chapter 11

A Grand Day for Gromit

Wallace and Gromit are cartoon characters whose films include *A Grand Day Out, A Close Shave, The Wrong Trousers* and *Cracking Contraptions*. Many of the original clay models and film sets were destroyed in a fire at the Aardman animation studios in 2005. In this article, Catherine Shoard wonders who the real fans of the cartoon pair might be.

Extract

1　There was no cheese. There were no cracking contraptions. No giant killer-bunnies showed up, and no one appeared to have put on the wrong trousers. But it was still a grand day out at the Animation Gallery in London last week, when fans travelled from far and wide (well, Yorkshire, mostly) to buy Wallace &
5　Gromit goodies and get them signed by the creator, Nick Park, fresh from bagging his fourth Oscar,[1] with Steve Box, director of the latest W&G movie: *The Curse of the Were-Rabbit.*
　　But these weren't just any old goodies – the stuff on sale was artwork, with price tags to match. None of the limited-edition prints available was priced at
10　less than £95; most were close to £300. *More Alluring Gromit*, a framed print

[1] Oscar: award from American film industry

Extract continued

of Gromit doing his best to add some sex-appeal to the huge fake female were-rabbit he's operating, could have been yours for just £225. Framed pics of Lady Tottington, Wallace's posh love interest, of dastardly Victor Quartermaine, of Gromit's first birthday, of Wallace drinking tea, were also available.

15   They were big and bright and funny. They'd look fab on your bedroom wall, above the box of Meccano, maybe, or the My Little Ponies. But children were barely in evidence last Thursday. Of the 300 or so people crammed into the gallery, only about 15 were of school age, the rest were well advanced into adulthood. James, a smartly suited thirty-something from London, spoke with
20   pride about his collection of stills from previous W&G films, as well as from *Roobarb and Custard* and *Dangermouse*. He'd snapped up a *More Alluring Gromit* and another of Gromit in his greenhouse measuring his prize marrow – it reminded him, he said, of his father. No, he wasn't a collector, 'but if the pictures appreciate in value, that's a bonus.'

25   Paul, a jolly gent who'd travelled down from Lancashire, was also a multiple buyer, and highly savvy on the price of W&G wallpaper on eBay. Vince from Kent had brought along his children, Abby, eight, and Teddy, four, but they seemed rather less enthusiastic than Daddy. Vince's most prized collectable was actually a model of Mr Tweedy's dog from another Nick Park
30   feature, *Chicken Run*. Rare, eh, considering the fire at Aardman HQ in 2005? Yeah, well, he got it from a contact.

    Others were lower-key fans. Elizabeth and John, a middle-aged couple from Crawley, were getting out their cheque book for a *More Alluring Gromit*. As was Paul from Huddersfield, Maureen from Leeds, Bung from Stevenage, John
35   from Bournemouth and his brother, Mark, from Heathrow.

    It was startling just how much more popular Gromit was than Wallace. No one seemed to prefer the dairy-loving inventor to his mute pooch. A picture of Gromit finding some bunnies in the fridge was highly sought after. Liz and Abby from Eastbourne were buying one. Kim from London was buying two –
40   one for herself and one for her brother, to hang in his new kitchen.

    But the immense appeal of *More Alluring Gromit* was most revealing. Many of the fans were keen to claim that Wallace & Gromit has much adult content, that it works on levels only grown-ups can appreciate. But this seems like wishful thinking. Could it be that forking out hundreds of pounds on a picture
45   of a cartoon character is easier to justify if you insist it's a subtle piece of art, not just a giggle for kids?

    The few children that were present offered rather more frank comments on the appeal of W&G. 'It's funny,' said Catherine, eight, from Stoke Newington, there with her mum, Trudi. As did Charlotte, 11, whose mother, Carolyn, had

50   won a competition to meet Nick Park on BBC Radio Essex. (Question: What's Wallace's favourite cheese?)

Most heartfelt was the response of Zoe, six, from Skipton, clutching a ball of sweaty-looking Plasticine. 'Gromit is loyal. I'd like a dog like that. He'd be the best friend you'd ever have.'

Questions

1   Read lines 1–2 'There was no cheese . . . wrong trousers.' Explain clearly **two** ways in which the writer captures the reader's attention in these opening sentences of the passage, and explain how they are effective.   **4 A/E**

2   From details given in the first paragraph (lines 1–7), explain in your own words what sort of event was being held at the Animation Gallery in London.   **2 U**

3   Look at the first two sentences in the second paragraph: 'But these weren't . . . close to £300.'

   a)   In your own words explain what the writer found surprising about the merchandise on offer.   **1 U**

   b)   Show how the word choice and tone in this extract emphasises the contrast between what the writer expected to be on sale and what was actually on offer.   **4 A**

4   **a)**   What do the references to Meccano and My Little Ponies suggest about the kind of people the writer expected to be interested in Wallace and Gromit?   **1 U**

   b)   Show how the sentence 'But children were barely in evidence last Thursday' (lines 16–17) acts as a link in the argument at this point.   **2 U/A**

5   **a)**   The collector called James is described as 'a smartly suited thirty-something from London'. Suggest a reason why the writer included any of these details about him.   **2 A**

   b)   With close reference to lines 19–24, explain how far making money was important to James in collecting the Wallace and Gromit artwork.   **2 U**

6 Read again the story of Vince in lines 27–31. Quote **two** words or phrases which suggest an actual conversation taking place. **2 A**

7 In lines 32–35, the writer lists many of the buyers, calling them by their first names. What attitude to the buyers do you think this suggests? **1 A**

8 In line 32 he describes some fans as 'lower-key'. Explain how the image used here helps you understand what the writer means. **2 A**

9 Read lines 41–46: 'But the immense appeal . . . a giggle for kids?' Explain how the context helps you arrive at the meaning of the phrase 'wishful thinking' (line 44). **3 U**

10 Read lines 47–54. Explain what the writer's word choice and use of quotation reveal about her attitude to the children and their views. **4 A**

TOTAL MARKS: **30**

Taking a closer look . . .

Tone

What is meant by the **tone** is the way the writer's feelings or attitude to a topic are put across.

In the passage you have just read, the writer describes a sale of artwork from *Wallace and Gromit* cartoon films which attracted many more adults than children. The adults were taking it very seriously and paying a lot of money for the items on sale. Because the writer found this surprising and funny, the tone of much of the article is humorous.

In question 1, where you were asked how the writer captured the reader's attention, you could have suggested **a humorous tone** as one possible answer.

One way in which the writer achieves this is with references to ridiculous things from the Wallace and Gromit films, such as 'giant killer bunnies'.

What other attitudes might a writer express? The following box contains a checklist. In the examples that follow, try to decide which of these is the most appropriate in describing the writer's tone.

	Tone	
admiring	emotive (emotional and arousing emotion)	respectful
affectionate	humorous/joking	sarcastic
angry	ironic (saying the opposite of what you really mean)	serious
chatty	mocking	thoughtful
disrespectful	reflective	tongue-in cheek (pretending to take something seriously while slyly making fun of it)

For practice

Identify what you think the writer's **tone** is in each of the following extracts from the passage. Try to explain how the tone is achieved, for example through the use of techniques such as word choice, formal/informal expression, sentence structure, ideas etc. In each case you should **quote** the word(s) that contribute to the tone you have identified.

1 'fans travelled from far and wide (well, Yorkshire, mostly) to buy Wallace & Gromit goodies' (lines 4–5)

2 'a framed print of Gromit . . . could have been yours for just £225.' (lines 10–12)

3 'They'd look fab on your bedroom wall, above the box of Meccano, maybe, or the My Little Ponies.' (lines 15–16)

4 'Paul, a jolly gent who'd travelled down from Lancashire, was also a multiple buyer, and highly savvy on the price of W&G wallpaper on eBay.' (lines 25–26)

5 'Vince from Kent had brought along his children . . . but they seemed rather less enthusiastic than Daddy.' (lines 27–28)

Chapter 12

A Child Star Grows Up

In this article, David Amsden describes his interview with Macaulay Culkin, who became a millionaire at the age of 10 when he starred in the film *Home Alone*.

Extract

1 To be a child star is to be a permanent spectacle, a freak show, an eternal curiosity. Macaulay Culkin has been in only two films in the past 12 years and yet, as we walk to our restaurant table for lunch, people whisper, gawk, and forget to eat.

5 It doesn't help that, at 25, he still looks startlingly like he did 16 years ago in *Home Alone*, when he slapped aftershave on his pale cheeks, gave a bug-eyed shriek and became a star. 'To a lot of people I still am that kid,' he says. 'It's a blessing and a curse. I can go to any restaurant without a reservation, but while I'm there, everyone's gonna be staring.'

10 He's quick-witted and chatty, affable but also distant. He tells me repeatedly that he leads a 'simple, simple life,' spending his free time walking the dog, feeding the fish, cleaning the house, and cooking for his girlfriend. As for his career, he hasn't retired. But he refers to himself as 'not exactly the hardest-working actor'.

15   An understandable position, given his past. Raised with six siblings in a one-bedroom apartment, he started getting good roles at age eight and was a millionaire by 10, but his rapid ascent seemed less adorable the more people learned about his home life.

     His father, Kit, ruled the family – 'his kingdom', says Culkin – by
20   humiliation and physical abuse, eventually leaving the household. His mother filed a custody suit for him, which began a bitter public battle with Kit, and then Culkin had both his parents legally blocked from controlling his 17 million dollar fortune, a move that estranged him from his father, who Culkin 'thinks' lives in Arizona now. At 17, Culkin married the actress Rachel Miner; by 20 he
25   was divorced. When he was arrested just over a year ago for possession of marijuana, he was annoyed at being perceived as conforming to a type. 'You know, I'm a former child actor,' he says with a sarcastic chuckle. 'I'm supposed to be a lot more mixed up than I am.'

     Child actors are supposed to play two roles. As children, they portray an
30   artificially sweet version of childhood; as adults, they are expected to crack up. 'Yeah, it's funny,' says Culkin. 'A lot of people meet me and they're like, 'Why aren't you crazy?' He has now produced a book called *Junior*, a semi-fictional story of a former child star. 'Yes, it's me,' says Culkin, 'but no, it isn't, you know?'

35   If *Junior* has a clear theme, it's coping with fame. The book continually returns to the subject of Junior's relationship with his father, a figure who has much in common with Kit Culkin.

     There's not a flicker of emotion as Culkin speaks of his father; it's as if he's describing a character in a film. 'He would black out all the terrible things that
40   he did, and that hurt me more, because he'd go to bed at night thinking he was a good person. I knew from a very early age that I had better take notes on him,' he says. 'Notes on how not to be, notes on how I don't want to be when I grow up.'

     In a sense, Culkin has aged in reverse. 'I have a lot of growing up to do . . .
45   or a lot of growing down. I think that's probably more appropriate.' His childhood – work, pressure, fame, wealth, marriage, divorce – reads like a checklist of adult milestones. Now, he is enjoying a belated adolescence, not worrying about money, work or the future.

     The following night Culkin invites me to play pool with him. Of course,
50   being in the real world isn't always easy. As we play pool, a woman approaches, staring at him unapologetically. 'Um, I think you're staring at me,' Culkin finally says, causing the woman to snap out of her trance.

     'Oh, uh, is that Macaulay?'

Extract continued

'No, only on my good days.' As she vanishes, Culkin laughs. Usually when
55 he points out their gawking, people apologise and go on their way. Not in this
case. A few minutes later the woman is back.

'I didn't mean to scare you,' she snipes. 'And don't worry, you're not that
cute.'

Culkin shrugs.

Questions

1 Read lines 1–4. 'To be . . . forget to eat.' Explain why the reaction of
   the people in the restaurant to Macaulay Culkin was surprising to the
   writer.   **2 U**

2 In lines 7–8, Culkin calls his celebrity status 'a blessing and a curse'.
   How do the examples he gives in lines 8–9 help make this clear?   **4 U/A**

3 Culkin describes himself as 'not exactly the hardest-working actor'
   (lines 13–14). Explain his meaning and comment on the tone of
   Culkin's words.   **2 U/A**

4 Show how the last words in paragraph four: 'his rapid ascent seemed
   less adorable the more people learned about his home life' (lines
   17–18) act as a link in the structure of the argument.   **2 U/A**

5 Using quotation to illustrate your answer, show how the word choice
   and imagery in lines 19–24 ('His father, Kit . . . lives in Arizona now')
   help you understand the strained relationships within Culkin's family.   **4 A**

6 Show how the context helps you understand the word 'estranged' in
   line 23.   **2 U**

7 'Child actors are supposed to play two roles.' (line 29)

   a) What function does this sentence have in the paragraph in which
       it appears? (lines 29–34)   **1 A**

   b) In your own words, explain the 'two roles' which child actors are
       expected to play.   **2 U**

8 Read lines 32–37 'He has now . . . Kit Culkin.' Explain, with close
   reference to the text, how far the character of the child star in the
   book *Junior* seems to be based on Culkin himself.   **4 U**

75

9 'As if he's describing a character in a film' (lines 38–39) Explain how this comparison helps you understand how Culkin manages to deal with the difficult relationship with his father. **2 A**

10 'His childhood – work, pressure, fame, wealth, marriage, divorce – reads like a checklist of adult milestones'. (lines 45–47)

   a)   What is the function of the dashes in this sentence? **1 A**

   b)   Explain the effect of the writer's use of imagery in either 'checklist' or 'milestones'. **2 E/A**

11 'If *Junior* has a clear theme, it's coping with fame.' (line 35) The story of Culkin's encounter with the woman during his game of pool ends with the words 'Culkin shrugs'. How effective is this sentence in illustrating how Culkin 'copes' with the down side of his own fame? **2 E**

TOTAL MARKS: **30**

Taking a closer look . . .

Anecdotes and illustrations

In Close Reading, the word **illustration** has nothing to do with pictures. It means an example that helps make something clear.

In question 2, you were asked to explain how the examples in lines 8–9 clearly showed that Culkin's celebrity status was both 'a blessing and a curse' to him.

The examples were from his experience at restaurants. Being famous is 'a blessing' because he can get a table, even when a restaurant is officially 'full' and ordinary people would be turned away. However, it is also 'a curse' since, although he can always get into any restaurant, people will stare at him while he is there. We can imagine how embarrassing and annoying this must be, and how it must spoil his enjoyment.

An **anecdote** is a small story which acts as an illustration. Macaulay Culkin's encounter with the woman in the pool room is an example of an 'anecdote'. The story is there to illustrate how rudely some members of the public treat celebrities. It also reveals something about Macaulay Culkin himself, in the way he handled a difficult situation.

Writers will often use an anecdote to begin or end an article, since such stories are interesting and entertaining to the reader as well as having the function of making a point in the argument clear.

For practice

In each of the following examples you will be asked to explain how the illustrations/anecdotes help make a point clear. You might write down the answers or discuss them with a partner or group.

1 In the first sentence, the writer says that being a child star is to be 'a permanent spectacle, a freak show, an eternal curiosity'.

    a)   Explain what each of these phrases means.

    b)   Explain how the writer's personal experience of walking through a restaurant with Macaulay Culkin (lines 2–4) acts as a helpful illustration.

2 Macaulay Culkin was keen to convince the interviewer that he was just a normal person who leads a 'simple, simple life' (line 11). How far do the examples he gives in lines 11–12 help convince us this is true?

3 Read again the anecdote about the woman who interrupts the game of pool (lines 50–59).

    a)   Comment on the woman's behaviour and her words. (Think about 'staring at him unapologetically'; 'a few minutes later the woman is back'; 'she snipes'; "Don't worry, you're not that cute.")

    b)   What does her behaviour illustrate about the way some members of the public behave towards celebrities?

    c)   Comment on the way Macaulay Culkin speaks and acts in reaction to the woman. Try to identify the tone of his words. (In your answer you might refer to the following: "Um, I think you're staring at me"; 'Culkin *finally* says'; "No, only on my good days."; 'Culkin shrugs'.)

    d)   What do you think his reactions reveal about him as a person?

Chapter 13

A Life Lived on the Edge

In his reflections on a television documentary about the life of mountaineer Dougal Haston, journalist Jeremy Hodges considers the nature of men like Haston who risk their lives.

Extract

1   For those not bitten by the bug, it is hard to understand the appeal of going out in appalling weather, clinging to a rock face in sub-zero temperatures, courting death at every invisible foothold for the dubious distinction of standing on a peak where few or none have set foot before. However carefully one follows
5   safety procedures, mountaineering must be infinitely more hazardous to health than smoking and it is a wonder the Scottish Executive hasn't banned it as a politically incorrect activity.

Dougal Haston, one of the world's greatest mountaineers, was killed by an avalanche while skiing near his Swiss home in 1977 at the age of 36. All boys
10   like to climb but few engage in it with such skill and determination as Haston and his friends Jim Stenhouse and Eley Moriarty did while still at school in the 1950s in Currie, Midlothian.

In those days, the village was a grim, working-class community whose redeeming feature, in the eyes of the 'Currie boys', was a stone bridge carrying
15   a disused railway track by the Water of Leith, which cushioned their falls when they came unstuck from this impromptu artificial rock face. From there they graduated to the Pentlands and Glen Coe, where their early mentor, Jimmy Marshall, recalled the 17-year-olds steaming effortlessly up a gully with their old Army ice-axes and baggy anoraks.

20   It was with Robin Smith that Haston achieved his first really impressive feat, scaling the tough rock face on Ben Nevis known as the Bat. And it was with Smith that Haston first came spectacularly unstuck, plunging through the air before being brought up safely on the end of a rope. Smith himself would come unstuck permanently in a climbing accident that killed him at 23 – the first
25   of many mountaineering chums who preceded Haston to an icy Valhalla.[1]

Film footage of Haston in action seems remarkably plentiful and we were treated to many shots of him caked in snow, performing superhuman feats en route to near-impossible summits. But only the memory of his friends at Edinburgh University, where he nominally studied Philosophy, brought back to
30   life Haston's wildness when not on the mountains.

There was no escaping the fact that his fanatical devotion to climbing was matched only by his love of drinking and getting into punch-ups – presumably the best way he could find to live close to the edge in the refined surroundings of Edinburgh.

35   Likewise, he could be trouble in the Highlands. Dissatisfied with the green 'public lavatory' décor of the Scottish Mountaineering Club's hut in Glen Coe, he decided to redecorate it a tasteful custard yellow with curious red psychedelic designs, thus inciting the wrath of club custodian Malcolm Slesser, who banned him.

40   Having left university without sitting his degree, Haston set up a climbing school in Glen Coe, where the drinking continued unabated. After a long session one night at the Clachaig Inn, he insisted on driving his van back and hit a group of hikers in the dark. Instead of helping the injured, Haston fled the scene. When one hiker later died, he was sentenced to six months in Barlinnie,
45   plus a £15 fine, for manslaughter. Even his friends found it hard to justify his drunken folly and lack of outward remorse. But in the programme, his fellow climber Hamish MacInnes revealed the incident had left Haston with a terrible burden of guilt 'that bothered him till the day he died'.

This was not a documentary that dwelt on the troubled private life of the
50   taciturn Scot, which in a way robbed it of emotional impact. His climbing

[1] Valhalla: place where Vikings believed their heroes went after death

Extract continued

triumphs – the Eiger, Annapurna in the Himalayas and Everest with Chris
Bonington – impressed me with a sense of his astonishing determination and
powers of mental and physical endurance, but brought me no closer to him as a
human being.

55 Many of his friends could not be interviewed, having dropped like flies from
the rock faces around him, yet some of the survivors – including Doug Scott and
Bonington, who was almost in tears when interviewed, clearly loved Haston for
something more than his technical ability.

After an hour I had seen a lot of the mountains – but I had barely glimpsed
60 the man.

Questions

1 Read lines 1–7. In your own words, explain what the writer thinks is
the main aim of mountaineers.   **1 U**

2 Explain how the metaphor 'bitten by the bug' (line 1) helps you
understand the enthusiasm of keen mountaineers.   **2 A**

3 a) Why does the writer suggest that mountaineering might reasonably
be banned?   **1 U**

   b) In lines 5–6 the writer compares the effects of mountaineering to
smoking. Explain how this helps the reader appreciate the dangers
of the sport.   **2 A**

4 a) Explain what is meant by a 'redeeming feature' (line 14).   **2 U**

b) In what way was the bridge a 'redeeming feature' of Currie to Dougal Haston and his friends?   **2 U**

5 a) Identify a word from lines 13–19 which tells the reader that the railway bridge was not specially adapted for rock climbing.   **1 U**

b) Identify a word from lines 13–19 which tells us that climbing in the Pentlands and Glen Coe was more difficult than climbing the railway bridge.   **1 U**

6 'Jimmy Marshall recalled the 17-year-olds steaming effortlessly up a gully with their old Army ice-axes and baggy anoraks.' (lines 17–19) How does the writer's word choice create an effective contrast between the mountaineers' skill and their equipment?   **2 A**

7 Look again at the first sentence in paragraph five (lines 26–28): 'Film footage . . . summits.' Quoting **two** examples in your answer, explain how the writer's word choice in this sentence effectively expresses his admiration of Haston's talent.   **2 A**

8 In your own words, explain the reason the writer suggests in the sixth paragraph (lines 31–34) for Haston's love of drinking and 'getting into punch-ups'.   **2 U**

9 Explain the meaning and tone of the word 'tasteful' as the writer uses it in line 37.   **2 U/A**

10 Read again the account of the fatal accident in lines 40–48. Making detailed reference to the evidence given by the writer in these lines, explain in your own words what you think the incident reveals about Haston as a man.   **3 A**

11 Explain the function of the dashes in lines 51–52.   **1 A**

12 'Many of his friends could not be interviewed, having dropped like flies from the rock faces around him . . .' (lines 55–56) Suggest **two** reasons why the simile 'like flies' is particularly effective in this context.   **2 A**

13 The writer sums up his view of the TV programme by saying, 'After an hour I had seen a lot of the mountains – but I had barely glimpsed the man.' With close reference to the passage, explain how far you agree with the author that you have learned little about the personality of Dougal Haston.   **4 E**

TOTAL MARKS: **30**

Taking a closer look . . .

Emotive language

Emotive language is language that aims to arouse emotions in the reader. It expresses extremes of feeling. You may be asked to describe and analyse this technique.

For example, in the phrase 'appalling weather', the word 'appalling' is used to mean very bad. The verb to 'appal' means to shock and horrify. The idea is that the weather is so bad it shocks and horrifies you.

Using the word 'appalling' is more vivid and effective than the emotionally neutral expression 'very bad' as it is **emotive**: it arouses feeling in the reader.

In question 7, you were asked to explain the effectiveness of the writer's word choice in expressing the feeling of admiration. A good answer would recognise that words such as 'superhuman' and 'near-impossible' are emotive, as they both express and arouse feelings of awe and admiration.

For practice

Fill in the gaps in a copy of the table below. Firstly, analyse and comment on the effect of the original expression. You should mention features you notice such as metaphor or hyperbole (exaggeration) which contribute to the emotive effect.

Secondly, suggest an emotionally neutral alternative to the word or expression used in the passage.

Word or expression from the passage	Analysis of original expression and comment on effect	Emotionally neutral alternative
appalling (line 2)	Word suggests extreme feeling of shock or horror: weather is seen to be especially bad to arouse these feelings.	very bad
courting death (lines 2–3)		
superhuman (line 27)		
fanatical devotion (line 31)		
inciting the wrath (line 38)		
terrible burden of guilt (lines 47–48)		

Chapter 14

Germany's Grown Up

In this article, German journalist Thomas Kielinger suggests it is time to put aside the stereotypes of the past when we look at modern Germany.

Basil Fawlty from the television series 'Fawlty Towers'

Extract

1 Don't ask me to ditch my beloved stereotypes, please. What would jokes about national characteristics be without the topsoil of cliché, the milk of human unkindness? Let me share with you my favourite joke in this league. It is about Heaven and Hell, and how Europeans are allocated certain tasks according to

5 the national characteristics they are best known for.

Predictably, in Heaven, the chef is French, the policeman British, the mechanic German, the organiser Swiss and the lover Italian. In Hell, of course, the order is somewhat different. The chef is British, the policeman German, the mechanic French, the organiser Italian and the lover Swiss.

10 Quite apart from the intriguing question of why it's agreed that the Swiss are such bad lovers, the rest of the baddies' list hardly bears deep scrutiny, either. If I were a would-be mayhem plotter, I should not want to cross the path of a British anti-terrorist cop – who easily knocks the proverbial German policeman off his plinth as the most unforgiving guardian of the law. And as for

➤

15 the chef in Hell being British – why, the United Kingdom now has one of the most cosmopolitan cuisines anywhere.

And yet I would never advocate laying to rest such jokes – or even those about the Germans and the Second World War. Don't let anyone tell you that we get upset about that. We actually enjoy Basil Fawlty's 'Don't mention the 20 war' rant just as much as you do. Why? Because we can't get the last war out of our system either. German television is awash with renditions of that horrid chapter in our national history.

In fact, Basil Fawlty allows us, for once, the pleasure of actually laughing about it all, something we still can't quite muster of our own accord. Humour 25 is a vital tool in confronting evil.

But wait a minute, Germans do get upset about stereotypical jokes about the W word. The funny side escapes us if the Germany of the Nazis is confused with the Germany of today. There lies the rub. There is a distinct fire-break in our mind about then and now; between the swastika'd pariahs and the country 30 we have rebuilt 'with liberty and justice for all' – including the liberty to mock ourselves for the past descent into hell. By contrast, for too many Britons the old adversary has become frozen in time, encapsulated in 1945 like an insect in amber. This is where our paths diverge.

Germany has moved on, with a vengeance. The constant harping on a 35 happily extinct Germany – can it come from your post-war role as 're-educator' to a vanquished society? Is there, perhaps, still something of the schoolmaster in you, wanting to occasionally rap the Germans' knuckles? Well, don't worry. With stereotypical thoroughness we have imbibed the past and all its lessons. But there is no need to stand guard over Germany as if she were on probation.

40 Fortunately, people will see in the future a different Germany, the modern version, so relaxed, in fact, that its inhabitants have all but forgotten the work ethic they were once famous for. The fun society we call it. Chill out, and let the social net take care of you.

Well, I'd better stop here lest I indulge in some negative stereotyping of my 45 own.

Questions

1. Identify **one** technique used by the author to establish a conversational tone in the opening paragraph.   **1 A**

2. Read paragraph three (lines 10–16). Explain how the author's view of British chefs and German policemen differs from the stereotyped views.   **4 U**

3. Show how the rest of the sentence helps you understand the meaning of 'would-be mayhem plotter' (line 12).   **2 A**

4. In your own words, explain why the Germans enjoy Basil Fawlty's jokes about the war.   **2 U**

5. a) Explain what the author means by the phrase 'the W word' (lines 26–27). **1 U**

   b) Why is the phrase appropriate?   **1 A**

6. Which sentence in paragraph six (lines 26–33) helps the reader understand the kind of joke that Germans object to?   **1 U**

7. The dictionary defines 'fire-break' (line 28) as *a strip of open land near a forest designed to prevent a forest fire from spreading.* How effective is this word as an image or metaphor to describe the attitude of modern-day Germans to the Nazi period?   **2 A**

8. Read lines 28–31. In your own words, explain how the writer considers modern Germany to be different from Nazi Germany.   **2 U**

9. Read paragraph six again (lines 26–33).

   a) What criticism does the writer make of the British attitude to Germany? **1 U**

   b) Comment on any aspect of the word choice or imagery which helps to make this clear.   **2 A**

10 Quote an expression from paragraph seven (lines 34–39) which shows
    the author is pleased that 'Germany has moved on' from its past.   **1 A**

11 How effective is the expression 'something of the schoolmaster'
    (line 36) in describing the British attitude to Germany?   **2 A**

12 Read paragraph eight (lines 40–43).

    a) What does the writer consider the main characteristic of Germany
        is likely to be in the future?   **2 U**

    b) What danger does he see in this?   **1 U**

    c) How does the tone of 'Chill out, and let the social net take care of
        you' (lines 42–43) reveal the writer's attitude to this way of thinking? **2 A**

13 Explain, with close reference to the ideas and style of the passage,
    how effective the writer is in showing the Germans in a positive light.   **3 E**

TOTAL MARKS: **30**

Taking a closer look . . .

Using your own words

Question 4 begins, 'In your own words, explain . . .'

When answering questions in a Close Reading test, it is important that you try
to use your own words as far as possible in *all* the questions, *except* for those
that ask you to quote from the passage. (In the exercise 'Germany's Grown Up',
only questions 6 and 10 ask you to quote directly.)

Copying your answers directly from the passage is called 'lifting', and you are
likely to get no marks if you do this.

Certain questions, such as question 4, remind you of this rule. Examiners
include the reminder in questions where they feel you may be tempted just to
copy an answer.

> *Tip: Be especially careful of the questions marked **'U'** for **'Understanding'**. These
> are the questions where you are most likely to make this error.*

'But I can't always think of different words!'

It is not necessary to find an alternative for every single word. However, there are certain simple rules to follow:

- Do not lift phrases of three or more words – you may re-use single words.

- Never repeat a simile or metaphor – always express it simply.

- Never use slang or very informal language from the passage – always make your expression fairly formal.

- Avoid emotive language – try to use neutral expressions.

For practice (1)

In the passage, 'Germany's Grown Up', the writer uses a humorous, very individual style, full of informal expressions and figures of speech. Express the following extracts from the passage in your own words (some extracts are slightly adapted).

1 'Don't ask me to ditch my beloved stereotypes' (line 1)

2 Europeans are allocated certain tasks according to their national characteristics. (lines 4–5)

3 'the baddies' list hardly bears deep scrutiny' (line 11)

4 'one of the most cosmopolitan cuisines anywhere' (lines 15–16)

5 'that horrid chapter in our national history' (lines 21–22)

6 'Humour is a vital tool in confronting evil.' (lines 24–25)

7 'frozen in time' (line 32)

8 'This is where our paths diverge.' (line 33)

9 'constant harping on a happily extinct Germany' (lines 34–35)

10 Wanting to rap the Germans' knuckles (line 37)

For practice (2)

You might discuss these more difficult examples in pairs or groups. Your teacher or tutor may need to give you a clue in some examples. (Notice that most of these examples contain metaphors.)

1 Jokes about national characteristics have the topsoil of cliché, the milk of human unkindness. (lines 2–3)

2 The British cop easily knocks the German policeman off his plinth as the most unforgiving guardian of the law (lines 13–14)

3 'swastika'd pariahs' (line 29)

4 'we have imbibed the past and all its lessons' (line 38)

5 'Chill out, and let the social net take care of you.' (lines 42–43)

Chapter 15

London: a Timeless City

In this passage Catherine Nixey looks at how the city of London has developed over the centuries and analyses why the city has such an appeal.

Extract

1   The air is filled with sitar music, with the clucking of the birds being sold in cages, and with the smell of spices. Most of the signs, including the station sign, are in the curling Gurmukhi script of the Punjabi language. You are, of course, in Southall.

But take the train half an hour east and you would be in Piccadilly, one of
5   London's grandest and busiest areas. Massive stone buildings remind you that London was once the capital of an empire that covered a third of the globe. The beautiful and expensive shops remind you that it is still one of the richest cities in the world. St Paul's, Buckingham Palace, the Ritz, the Tate and the Houses of Parliament are all just a stone's throw away.

10   But were you to get back on the Tube and travel a little further, you would emerge in Epping Forest, a forest of beautiful oak trees and blackberry bushes.

It is difficult to come to terms with the scale or with the diversity of the area in and around the M25. Twelve million people live here. That's more than the populations of Norway and Denmark combined! And at the core is, of course,
15   the city of London.

London is a city of superlatives. It is not only Europe's largest city, but also its richest and its most ethnically diverse. What's more, Greater London, perhaps surprisingly, has more green spaces than any other city of its size in the world.

20 And to transport you around this massive metropolis are the famous red London buses and the infamous London Underground. When it was first built in 1863, the Tube was the world's first underground railway. The spaghetti of confusion is recognised and navigated by most through the much simplified and now iconic London Tube map, designed by Harry Beck in 1931.

25 London is currently booming. It has money, and it likes to spend. Shops, cafés, restaurants and bars across the city are permanently filled with Londoners having fun. And the prices are an indication of its prosperity. The average rent is, shockingly, 56 per cent more in the Greater London area than elsewhere in Britain. But rather than curb people's desire for the bright lights, the demand for
30 city revelry continues to rise, and Greater London's boundaries push further into the suburbs to cater for it. Greater London has most of the country's wealth – and it needs it.

It is extraordinarily rich in culture and history too. Here was where Guy Fawkes plotted, Isaac Newton did sums, The Beatles made records, the anti-
35 slavery lobby was founded, Oscar Wilde partied . . . And there were bigger events: Roman invasions, plagues, fires, Zeppelin bombings, air raids.

However, the culture and history don't stop at the city gates. Dotted around London are countless beautiful villages, and exquisite country houses. Like a well-aged face, Greater London's history shows in its lines. Some roads are
40 straight, echoing old Roman roads; others follow the contours of the old city wall. Hyde Park is only there because Henry VIII wanted somewhere to go hunting. St. Paul's Cathedral was built because the Great Fire of London had created the space, as well as the need for non-flammable buildings.

Its history as capital of the British Empire still moulds London today. After
45 the Second World War, there was a huge influx of Indian, Pakistani and Afro-Caribbean workers to the area from the colonies.

It is a place that has shaped the world, and that the world has shaped. Massive and intimate, traditional but ever-changing, hugely multicultural but ineffably British, Greater London is almost impossible to define – and almost
50 impossible to resist. The world is coming to London. You could do worse than follow it.

Questions

1 Explain how the author uses a variety of sense impressions in the description in the opening paragraph. **2 A**

2 Comment on the importance of the sentence 'You are, of course, in Southall' (line 3) to the effectiveness of the whole paragraph. **2 A**

3 State one contrast between the different areas of London described in paragraph two and paragraph three. **2 U**

4 Quote the word in paragraph four (lines 12–15) that sums up how much variety there is in London life. **1 U**

5 How does the writer help the reader to understand how large the population of London is? **2 A**

6 Explain the meaning of 'superlatives' (line 16) and show how the rest of the paragraph helps you to arrive at this meaning. **2 A**

7 a) Comment on how effective 'spaghetti of confusion' (lines 22–23) is as an image or metaphor. **2 A**

   b) Quote another word from this paragraph which continues the idea that the London Underground system can be difficult to use. **1 U**

8 'London is currently booming' (line 25). By referring to **two** examples, show how the author expands on this statement in the rest of paragraph seven (lines 25–32). **2 U/A**

9 Look at the sentence in lines 33–36. How does the structure of this sentence reinforce the idea that London is 'extraordinarily rich in culture'? **2 A**

10 'However, the culture and history don't stop at the city gates'. (line 37) Explain how this sentence is an appropriate link between the paragraph it begins and the previous one. **2 A**

11 a) 'Like a well-aged face, Greater London's history shows in its lines.' (lines 38–39) Explain the effectiveness of this comparison. **2 A**

    b) Give **two** examples of how London's history has affected the position of buildings or the layout of streets. **2 U**

12 In your own words, explain **two** of the contrasts mentioned in the last paragraph to be found in present-day London life. **2 U**

13 How successful is the writer in persuading you that London is 'almost impossible to resist'? Identify at least **two** literary techniques that help to convince the reader of London's appeal. **4 E**

TOTAL MARKS: **30**

Taking a closer look . . .

Imagery

Almost every Intermediate and Higher Close Reading paper contains a question like number 7a above:

Comment on how effective 'spaghetti of confusion' (lines 22–23) is as an image or metaphor.

The term 'image' is used to refer to a descriptive word or phrase that involves some kind of comparison. It is likely to involve one of three figures of speech:

Simile	Metaphor	Personification
a comparison between two different things using the word 'as' or 'like'. ('A is like B')	a comparison where instead of saying that 'A is like B' the writer says 'A <u>is</u> B'.	a specific type of metaphor comparing an inanimate object to a living thing.

To explain why an image is a good one, you should try to think how the comparison sheds light on the subject under discussion.

One class, when asked what they associated with 'spaghetti', came up with the following suggestions:

- Something Italian

- A tangled mess

- Long thin strips of pasta

- Stuff mixed together

Which of these connotations of the word 'spaghetti' do you think the writer had in mind when she used the metaphor 'spaghetti of confusion' to describe the London Underground map?

For practice

1 The following extract describes the attractions of Morocco as a tourist destination. Examples of imagery are underlined.

- Identify each image as a simile, metaphor or personification.

- Work out what is compared to what.

- Discuss how the two are similar.

1 From urban breaks and seaside escapes to week-long treks, Morocco is an exciting and varied destination. <u>Adrenalin junkies</u> have various options: the Atlantic seaboard offers fantastic surfing opportunities; east of Marrakesh, the Todra Gorge presents word-class rock-climbing; and the desert is perfect for
5 off-piste driving over <u>sugar-soft</u> sand dunes. Arrange a camel safari and head out for a night under <u>crystal-clear</u> skies.

(Source: *Wanderlust*, Issue 73, August 2005)

2 This extract describes a trip to the Grand Canyon in the USA. Again, identify the underlined images as similes, metaphors or personification and comment on how effective these comparisons are.

1 The heat in Arizona is legendary. The land is so parched that each step throws up <u>clouds</u> of orange dust. When a chain of tethered pack-horses passed us coming the other way we were temporarily lost in <u>an orange fog</u>.
   As we descend, the Canyon walls grew evermore imposing and I felt that
5 we were in the <u>middle of a battleground fought over by armies of cacti</u>. Rocks and boulders hemmed us in <u>like giant towers</u>. Sun and shade gave them definition and shape: here a <u>grizzly bear of granite</u>; there <u>a troupe of acrobatic sandstone dolphins</u>.

Eventually we reached the first of the falls. Havasu is a classic, symmetrical,
10 25 metre plume: poised, refined and self-consciously beautiful. I walked down
the path beside her and looked back up. If you blink quickly enough the water
appears to stop: giant drops suspended, like a theatre-curtain of water, reluctant
to fall until the thunderous applause dies down. It never does, of course. Havasu
Falls is sourced by an underground spring, its volume and temperature
15 consistent year round. The waterfall is its own everlasting and thunderous
ovation.

(Source: *Wanderlust*, Issue 75, November 2005)

Chapter 16

Eat Up and Pay Up

Journalist Giles Coren recently made a TV programme on obesity which came up with the controversial idea of taxing people in proportion to how overweight they are. Here, he reflects on some aspects of obesity which came to him while researching the programme.

Eddie Murphy starred as the overweight Professor Sherman Klump in 'The Nutty Professor'

Extract

1   How many fat people have you seen today? Did the milkman waddle down your garden path on legs like giant kebabs? Did the chap in the newsagent where you bought your paper puff and sweat as he put your money in the till with his podgy hand? Perhaps you yourself are – how can I put this politely? – 'fuller-
5   figured'? In which case, you may want to stop reading now. As for the rest of you, stop looking so smug. Because has it ever occurred to you that porkers aren't just putting pressure on their elasticated waistbands – they're costing the whole country money as well?

And the bill is not just a few pounds here and there to repair a broken park
10   bench or the odd public loo seat. I should stress at this point that there is a tiny percentage of people with genuine metabolic problems that cause them to pile on the pounds. They, of course, deserve sympathy rather than contempt. But the

vast majority of chubbies in Britain are big because they lack the willpower or incentive to maintain a healthier lifestyle. We're paying for their self-indulgence.

15   Last year, treatment of obesity-related illnesses cost the National Health Service – wait for it – £1 billion. Another £2.5 billion was lost to the economy on account of premature death, sick pay and incapacity benefits related to obesity. There are 900 people in Britain so fat that they can do, almost literally, nothing at all. These super-whoppers cost the country £8 million just on their
20   own.

And where does this money – almost £4 billion – come from? From the taxes paid by thin, healthy people like me. And I'm sorry, but I just don't think it's fair. Smokers are expected to pay vast amounts in tax to fund their habit. Boozers are taxed in the same way; gamblers, too. And I think it's high time the
25   obese were made to stump up as well. The time has come to tax the fat. An individual's tax bill would be tailored to reflect their girth.

I've just finished filming a TV documentary in which I travelled the land talking to health experts, politicians and economists about the fat crisis. I spent time listening to the overweight justify their size. I even wore a fat suit in public
30   for two days to gauge other people's reactions (never again – the stigma was unbearable).

Fat people tell me that I am prejudiced and that the overweight are a 'minority group' as deserving of respect as any other. I beg to differ. Being fat is a choice. A choice to consume dwindling resources, to use more energy, to
35   take up more space. The fat people I interviewed for the film were always telling me they couldn't change their size. A moment's research soon proved this was tosh. People said: 'I'm not fat. I'm just big-boned.' Nonsense. Have you ever seen a fat skeleton? They said, 'I've got a slow metabolism.' Piffle. Fat people, if anything, have higher metabolisms than the rest of us because of
40   the amount of effort it takes to haul their bulk around. They told me, 'It's genetic'. Poppycock. What fat children inherit from fat parents is bad eating habits, not fat bellies. They said, 'Obesity is a disease of the poor. They cannot afford to eat healthily'. How patronising.

I debunked this myth by taking £20 (the bottom end of what a person on the
45   minimum wage or standard benefits spends on food in a week) and buying more than enough healthy food to last seven days. I bought pounds of fresh vegetables (carrots, cabbage, beans), two pounds of organic beef, two salmon steaks, four pounds of whole wheat pasta, two pounds of porridge, two pints of semi-skimmed organic milk, bags of pulses, four tins of tomatoes, two sacks of
50   oranges and a sack of apples. Why do people instead prefer to spend £20 on two giant takeaway pizzas and a lethal torpedo of fizzy pop?

Extract continued

The obesity crisis in Britain is a product of the terrible clash between the victim mentality and the 'Oprah culture' that says we must be proud of what we are whatever we are. Dawn French, the actress, is a classic example. She
55 recently claimed she was a better role model than skinny supermodels who, she said, encourage girls to be anorexic. But she is wrong. Massive deviation from the normal body shape is unhealthy and dangerous whichever direction you go in.

They are simply two sides of the same coin. Her insistence that a woman
60 can be fat and beautiful is fair enough. And she was a good example of this for many years. But she is now huge, in imminent danger of terrible health breakdown, and to encourage young women to think that this is acceptable is irresponsible in the extreme.

We must make people aware of the damage they are doing to their health by
65 being grossly overweight. And by far the most effective way to do this is to hit them where it hurts – in their wallets. It worked with smoking. And I firmly believe it would work with obesity.

Britain is dying of fat. And while tax may be a bitter pill for tubbies to swallow (nothing like as yummy as an extra helping of treacle pud) I believe
70 it's the only cure that will work.

Questions

1   From the first two sentences (lines 1–2), identify **two** techniques the writer has used to capture the interest of the reader.   **2 A**

2   Suggest a reason why the writer uses the expression 'fuller-figured' rather than 'fat' in lines 4–5.   **1 A**

3   Whom does the writer mean by 'the rest of you' in lines 5–6?   **1 U**

4   Look again at the second sentence of paragraph two, 'I should stress . . . pounds.'

   a)   How does the tone of this sentence differ from that used in the passage up to this point?   **1 A**

   b)   Explain clearly, using examples, how the writer's word choice in this sentence creates this tone.   **2 A**

5   From what the writer says in the second paragraph (lines 9–14), explain in your own words what he believes are the main reasons for people to be overweight.   **2 U**

6 Suggest a reason why the writer uses the word 'we' rather than 'tax-payers', for example, in the expression 'We're paying for their self-indulgence.' (line 14)   **2 A**

7 Show how the writer uses sentence structure effectively in lines 15–16: 'Last year . . . billion.'   **2 A**

8 Explain **two** ways in which the writer conveys his attitude to the '900 people . . . so fat they can do, almost literally, nothing at all' (lines 18–19).   **2 A**

9 In lines 21–26, 'And where . . . girth' the writer compares obese people to three other groups of people. Suggest a reason why obese people might be compared to any **one** of these other groups.   **2 U**

10 In your own words explain the meaning of the last sentence of paragraph four: 'An individual's . . . girth' (lines 25–26).   **2 U**

11 In paragraph six the writer sets out to dismiss the arguments that claim fat people cannot change their size. Show how he uses both sentence structure and word choice effectively to do this in lines 37–43.   **4 A**

12 Read lines 44–51. Explain briefly how the writer 'debunked the myth' that poor people cannot eat healthily.   **1 U**

13 Explain in your own words why the writer feels Dawn French was wrong to say she is a better role model than the 'skinny supermodels'.   **2 U**

14 The writer's message in this article is that fat people deserve to be taxed more than thin people. Looking at the article as a whole, explain how effective you found the writer's style and arguments in putting across this message.   **4 E**

TOTAL MARKS: **30**

Taking a closer look ...

Evaluation (1): evaluating the whole passage

The final question in this exercise asks you how **effective** Giles Coren has been in persuading you that fat people deserve to pay more tax than thin people.

The code letter **'E'** for **'Evaluation'** after a question tells you that you will be asked for an appreciation of how effective the writer has been in achieving his purpose, whatever it may be. Some evaluation questions may ask you to focus on a particular part of the passage, such as the conclusion, while others will require you to look at the passage as a whole.

- In Evaluation questions, you may include material that has already been discussed in the Understanding and Analysis questions.

- Look carefully at the number of marks available. It is a good idea to include one quotation / close reference followed by a comment on it for each mark available.

- Think about the writer's purpose. Is it to persuade, or to provoke thought, or to be humorous, for example? The point of Evaluation questions is to consider how well the writer has achieved it.

Hint: The pieces of writing in the Close Reading tests will have been chosen by examiners because they believe they *are* effective. It is always advisable to respond **positively**. Candidates who try to argue that the writers are *not* effective give themselves a harder task!

Plan your answer: The best way to approach an evaluation question is to write brief notes first, perhaps in the form of quotations. Getting into the habit of planning your answer in this way will also stand you in good stead when you come to the more complex evaluation questions in Higher English.

In the passage you have just read, the writer's purpose was **to persuade.**

Question 14 was worth four marks. It asked for comments on both style and arguments. To make sure you answered the whole question, you might have made notes in the form of a table like this:

Style	Arguments
• 'legs like giant kebabs' (humour/ridicule) • Use of first person 'we' (involves reader)	• High cost of treatment of obesity-linked illnesses: £1 billion; other related problems. • £2.5 billion (precise statistics, very large sums). • Other groups with self-inflicted problems – drinkers, gamblers, etc. – have to pay (which is unfair).

Your answer might then have read like this:

> **Arguments:** The writer's arguments are effective. Using statistics such as '£1 billion' and '£2.5 billion' impresses on the reader the enormous amounts of money fat people cost the country. Another effective argument is that other groups such as drinkers and gamblers must pay for their addictions, which persuades the reader that it would be fair for fat people to pay also.
>
> **Style:** The writer uses humour effectively, e.g. 'legs like giant kebabs', to mock fat people for the state they have got themselves into. He uses 'we' rather than a more impersonal word like 'tax-payers' to arouse the reader's indignation that they, too, must pay.

Using sub-headings like those underlined above makes it easy for the marker to see what you have done. In this case, there are clearly two points made (with quotations or direct references) for each heading, and so the answer would definitely be awarded 4/4 marks.

For practice

Extend your table of notes above to include a further four to six points under each heading.

Style	Arguments
•	•
•	•
•	•
•	•

In addition to entering a quotation or reference, try to include a brief comment also, as in the examples above.

Remember that the examiner will *not* look at your plan. In the test, there is no need to draw tables carefully or write neatly – your plan and notes need only to be understood by you! Do them as quickly and briefly as possible – you will still reap the benefit as your answer will be clear and well supported.

Chapter 17

Chav-Air

In this article, writer Andrew O'Hagan argues that making travel by air cheaper may also cheapen the experience of flying in the negative sense.

Extract

1 The worst place in Britain used to be well known: it was the 11.15 overnight coach from Glasgow Buchanan Street to London St Pancras.

The journey would start with quiet men in duffle coats and students with knapsacks, all engaged in private thoughts or puzzles, but by the time the coach
5 was passing the lights of Carlisle – and a symphony of Special Brew cans had gone kss, kss, kss – the bus would resemble Bruegel's triumph of Death and you'd promise yourself that if necessary you'd steal the money for the plane next time.

Not any more.

10 The days when taking a British domestic flight was considered quite a posh thing to do are gone, and a journey with any of those cheap providers (collective name Chav-Air) is an experience best left to people who find themselves immune to extremely obnoxious environments. The other day I was flying to Inverness to attend a wedding. I knew it would be a drinking affair (it was), and
15 I knew I would be unafraid of the bottle (sadly true), but even that didn't help

me cope with the fact that there were people drinking pints of lager in the departure lounge at 7.30 in the morning.

The breakfast plates were piled with radioactive scrambled egg and heaps of carcinogenic sausages, but that didn't stop people lining up with their
20 buggies to buy them. Then you go downstairs and are kept waiting in some nylon-carpeted hell-hole while a woman with a squeaky voice tells you she's sorry for the inconvenience caused. The plane comes in an hour late from Prague and nobody's got a guaranteed seat so you end up sitting miles from your girlfriend who doesn't like flying, but who ends up sitting between two
25 Kit-Kat chomping nutcases who wonder if there are any scratchcards on board. (Of course, there are.)

Then come the dodgy perfume and the Cup-a-Soup. Then come the 'partnerships' with rubbishy hotels and car-hire firms. By this time you're wondering whatever happened to the great Edwardian ideal of luxurious and
30 thoughtful travel. 'Pack them in and sell them cheap' might be a rather democratising principle, but only if you're not thinking about what you're losing for your great saving. There are some things – books, and seats on aeroplanes – which can't be sold like cans of beans without the purchaser's experience of them becoming narrowed and limited and finally destroyed. This
35 is a difficult truth, and one that the degradation of air travel in this country attests to like nothing else.

Nowadays, the best way to travel is in the nice bit of the train (and Weekend First is a brilliant deal, where you get to upgrade for £15). The staff seem happy at their work, the tea comes in crockery and the drinks in glasses, a newspaper
40 is available, and you get the general impression that the idea is not to squeeze money out of you but to give you value for the money you've already spent. That is an older (and more genuinely democratising) spirit than the cheap airlines have adopted, where the airline sees itself as a kind of fast-food joint with propellers.

45 I also wonder what the ghastly cheap flights are really doing for their many destinations. If you talk to publicans in Dublin, you'll find they bemoan the 'Ryanair generation', guys hopping over the sea for stag nights, and many hotels have put a ban on crowds of young men coming in from the airport. If you flood those cities with people just looking for a change of pub, what then is
50 the difference between Bratislava and Bilboa, Turin and Edinburgh?

It used to be thought that the journey towards a place became part of your experience of it, and that travelling itself was an art, something that could enhance a sense of personal growth, or contribute to it. Now one might shudder at the idea of Easyjetting it to Venice, or Krakow, or Valencia. I'd also hazard

---

Extract continued

55 that those cities are busy shuddering themselves: it's hard to imagine that increased numbers of cut-price tourists do much to enrich the coffers of the Academia.[1]

It's a side issue in the new, thoroughly and cheaply accessible Europe: the way these destinations are increasingly less like themselves and more like one
60 another. You don't have to walk far in Berlin to find an 'English-style' breakfast; you can't avoid a Novotel or 'Paris-look' brasserie in Gdansk; and everywhere you go in any city you'll see fake Irish pubs.

Cheapness and familiarity have become the new watchwords of travel, and gone – or going – are the notions of peace, and exploring and adaptation. I hate
65 cheap flights because they actually cheapen the experience of going away. I am reliably informed that more and more people now choose to holiday within Britain, travelling in the comfort of their own cars. One must imagine they are running away from queues and scratchcards and apologies for the inconvenience caused. I can't say I blame them. And the next time I go to
70 Inverness, I'll let the train take the strain.

[1] Academia: famous art gallery in Venice

Questions

1 Using evidence from lines 3–8, explain how the behaviour of the passengers changed in the course of the journey. **2 U**

2 '. . . a symphony of Special Brew cans had gone kss, kss, kss . . .'
(lines 5–6) Comment on the effectiveness of any aspect of the writer's word choice here. **2 A**

3 Explain clearly the effect the writer achieves with the use of brackets in paragraph four (lines 10–17). **2 A**

4 Re-read paragraph five (lines 18–26). How does the writer's word choice help the reader to understand his opinion of the food available at breakfast? **2 A**

5 In your own words, explain **two** other ways in which the flight was an unpleasant experience. **2 U**

6 What is the effect of the repetition of the words 'then come' in line 27? **2 A**

7 '"Pack them in and sell them cheap" might be a rather democratising principle' (lines 30–31).

   What contrast do you notice in the author's style of expression in this sentence? **2 A**

8 How effective do you find the simile in line 33 in conveying the author's dislike of cheap air travel? **2 A**

9 In your own words, give **two** reasons why the writer feels that the train is 'the best way to travel' (line 37). **2 U**

10 What aspect of rail travel does the writer feel is more genuinely democratic than travelling with budget airlines? **2 U**

11 'I also wonder what the ghastly cheap flights are really doing for their many destinations.' (lines 45–46)

   Show how the rest of paragraph eight expands on the point made in this sentence. **2 A**

12 Comment on the effectiveness of the choice of the word 'flood' (line 49) in strengthening the author's argument against cheap flights. **2 A**

13 Comment on the effectiveness of any aspect of the author's punctuation in paragraph ten (lines 58–62). **2 A**

14 How appropriate do you find the last three sentences 'One must imagine . . .' (lines 67–70) as a conclusion to the article? **2 A**

15 How far has the author succeeded in convincing you of the disadvantages of cheap flights? **2 E**

TOTAL MARKS: **30**

Taking a closer look . . .

Evaluation (2): evaluating the conclusion

Evaluation questions, which are marked by the letter 'E', ask you to consider how effective you think the writer has been.

Some Evaluation questions will require you to look at the passage as a whole, but others may ask you to focus on a particular part of the passage. The conclusion of a passage is frequently chosen as a focus, as in the example of question 14 above.

In Chapter 16, which looked at evaluation of the whole passage, you were advised to answer evaluation questions *positively*, since the passages will have been chosen because they are effective. The same advice applies when answering questions on evaluating parts of a passage.

Look at an example:

> *How appropriate do you find the last three sentences as a conclusion to the article?*

To evaluate a conclusion successfully, you must show clear links between the conclusion and the rest of the article. As in the case of an evaluation of a whole passage, it is advisable to begin with a brief plan.

A good way to do this is in the form of a diagram, showing how the ideas and style of the conclusion relate back to the rest of the passage.

Feature	Conclusion	Rest of passage
• List of irritating aspects	• 'queues and scratchcards and apologies for inconvenience'	• kept waiting in 'nylon-carpeted hell-hole' (line 21); 'Kit-Kat chomping nutcases' (line 25)
• Blunt comments	• 'I can't say I blame them.'	• 'ghastly' (line 45)
• Expresses opinion: that trains are better than planes	• 'let the train take the strain' (humorous tone)	• Train is best way to travel (line 37)

The plan shows three bullet points making comparison between the conclusion and the whole passage. Since the question is worth 2 marks, this is more than sufficient to ensure you will get full marks for the question.

Remember to use words like 'reinforces', 'effective' and 'appropriate' throughout your answer. A suitable final version appears on the following page.

The list of irritating aspects: 'queues and scratchcards and apologies for inconvenience' uses a serious tone to refer back to his earlier more jocular complaints of the delay he endured in the 'nylon-carpeted hell-hole', sitting next to the 'nutcases' with scratchcards. This reinforces his list of dislikes.

'I can't say I blame them' is simple and blunt, as were expressions like 'ghastly' which he used earlier to convey his feelings effectively.

The final sentence, saying he will 'let the train take the strain' is appropriate as it returns to the humorous tone used throughout the passage by adapting an advertising jingle. He repeats his opinion that the train is better than flying, thus providing an appropriate conclusion to the article.

This is a very full answer in order to illustrate the method, and you would have gained the 2 marks by covering only two of the linked bullet points in the plan.

For practice

Answer the following question, using the guidelines above. Compile a plan using a simple grid form, and then write out your answer in sentences. Notice that this question is worth 4 marks, and so you should find at least four pairs of linked points to ensure that you get full marks.

Comment on the effectiveness of the last paragraph (lines 63–70) as a conclusion to the whole passage. 4 E

Conclusion	Rest of passage
•	•
•	•
•	•
•	•

Writing in Focus (2)

On page 7 of this book is a checklist of the kind of language features often asked about in Close Reading questions.

Now that you have worked through the practice papers you should be much more familiar with these features.

To test your progress, in this final exercise (which can be done in pairs or groups) you should try to identify as many examples of interesting language techniques as you can, and discuss the effects the writer is aiming for.

You can look back to the checklist on page 7 to remind you of what to look for, but no further hints are given here!

Extract

Nothing, and I Mean Nothing, is Better Value than This

Jeremy Clarkson drives the Daihatsu Charade

1   The best value thing I can think of at the moment is Daihatsu's new Charade. At £5,995 this is a car you can buy with your Switch card, on a whim, because the bus was late and there weren't any taxis and you couldn't be bothered to wait any longer.
    Don't think, however, that because the new Charade is cheap it's equipped
5   like a Turkish prison. You get antilock brakes, electronic brake force distribution, two airbags, speed-sensitive power steering, electric front windows, electric door mirrors, central locking and a CD player.

You also get a fair bit of oomph. Daihatsu, the first Japanese car maker to set up a shop in Britain back in 1965, has built a reputation for squeezing amazing power from very small spaces. I believe its old Charade GTti was in 1987 the world's most powerful one litre car.

Well, it has switched emphasis now with astonishing results. The three-cylinder one litre engine found in the new Charade has 12 valves, dynamic variable valve timing and twin overhead camshafts, all of which is very dull.

The results aren't, though. Official figures suggest it will do 68.9 mpg out of town, making this the most economical and the cleanest petrol-engined four-seater money can buy.

I was expecting it to move with the zest of a Saturday shop girl but no: 0 to 62 was dispensed within 12.2 sec and at one point on our test track I hit the ton. For a city car the Charade is amazingly lively.

I'm going to stick my neck out here. We often talk about which car has the best engine. The BMW M3's is very good but the Ferrari 360's V8 cannot be ignored. Nor can the VTEC motor in a Honda S2000. Honestly, though, all things considered, as a technical tour de force you're hard pressed to do better than the low-friction twin-cam in this Charade. It even makes a growly grrrrrrr sound.

So, good engine and good value for money, where's the drawback? Well, it's not what you'd call a large car. I've seen bigger handbags, in fact. But that's okay.

Nobody dreams of buying a smaller television set in the same way that none of you will dream of swapping whatever you've got now for a smaller car, no matter how clever it is at maths and stuff.

Old people, however, are different. Old people do think about getting a smaller house and a smaller garden. And they may very well want a smaller car because they only ever need to get from the beetle drive to the bridge club. So, Enid and Gilbert, this one's for you.

It's as easy to get into and out of as an easy chair. There's enough space in the back for a game of whist. So far as reliability's concerned the Charade will be exemplary. You're more likely to be let down by your kitchen table.

The best bit, though, I've saved till last. It's a remarkably comfortable car, soaking up speed humps and potholes with a disdain that belies the shortness of its wheelbase. Sure, on a racetrack it handles about as badly as any car I've ever driven, but who cares? My dog can't do the ironing – that's not what it's for.

When you turn it on, a readout on the dash says 'Hello, happy'. And when you turn it off, it says: 'See you – goodbye'. Obviously I'd smash that with a hammer, and then I'd be left with an easy-to-drive, super-comfortable, super-value, spacious, practical, economical city car that does motorways too.

Most of all, though, I'd be left with something unusual these days: something that costs less than you'd imagine.